Sufficiency: Historic Essays on the Sufficiency of Scripture

Heath Lambert, Wayne Mack, Doug Bookman, and David Powlison

ISBN: 1537391348
ISBN-13: 978-1537391342

Contents

Introduction   7
Heath Lambert

1   What is Biblical Counseling?   10
Wayne Mack

2   The Word of God and Counseling   41
Doug Bookman

3   The Sufficiency of Scripture to Diagnose and Cure Souls   94
David Powlison

4   Counsel the Sufficient Word   121
Heath Lambert

Introduction
Dr. Heath Lambert

The essays included in the book you are holding are intended to commemorate the 40th anniversary of the Association of Certified Biblical Counselors (ACBC). Founded in 1976 under the name of the National Association of Nouthetic Counselors (NANC), our purpose was to pursue excellence in biblical counseling by certifying individuals and institutions who knew how to engage in counseling and counseling training at an exemplary level. Over the last four decades, much has changed: our membership has grown significantly, we have changed our name, and our headquarters has moved from Pennsylvania to Indiana to Kentucky, and now to Florida. But the most important qualities about us have remained the same.

In particular, we are characterized by the same theological commitments that have undergirded our approach to counseling since our founding. One of the most central theological commitments that has defined our ministry is our dedication to the sufficiency of Scripture for counseling. All the members of our association are required to believe, as a condition of their certification, that the Scriptures of the Old and New Testament exert a comprehensive authority on the work we do in counseling ministry.

We are serious about the doctrine of the sufficiency of Scripture because without it the biblical counseling movement cannot exist. There are plenty of secular counselors who believe there is no place for the teaching of Scripture in counseling. There are also plenty of conservative evangelical Christians who love the Bible but believe it is a revelation of limited scope, which is not sufficient for counseling. Only authentically biblical counselors believe that faithful counseling is impossible without the Bible.

The inspired Scriptures alone reveal God's understanding of what is wrong with us, explains who we are supposed to be, and shows how God intends to change us through the work of our precious Redeemer, Jesus Christ. And so, by God's grace, our commitment to Scripture continues because we are convinced that apart from it we cannot help the people we are called to help, and our movement cannot—indeed, it should not—endure.

The doctrine of the sufficiency of Scripture is crucial to our movement, and is also what has made us so controversial to others who contend for different approaches to counseling. A doctrine so central and so debated has required constant defense by the leaders of our movement. Some of the most important works to come out of the biblical counseling movement have been the literature explaining and defending the sufficiency of Scripture. I am eager to celebrate our 40th anniversary, our rich theological tradition, and our commitment to Scripture by publishing a special edition of some of my favorite articles on sufficiency that have been published throughout the years.

Only one of the chapters in this commemorative book is original. It is the one by me. I wrote it in honor of our association's anniversary, and I pray that the Lord uses it to advance the cause of Christ through biblical counseling. The other chapters are contributed by men made of better stuff than I. These authors are luminaries who have shaped generations of biblical counselors through their teaching and writing.

Wayne Mack's chapter, "What Is Biblical Counseling?" was originally published in *Totally Sufficient: The Bible and Christian Counseling* edited by Ed Hindson and Howard Eyrich. I remember reading this chapter in my church office when it occurred to me that, before then, I had never read a more persuasive argument about the sufficiency of Scripture. Douglas Bookman's chapter, "The Word of God and Counseling" was originally published in

Introduction to Biblical Counseling edited by John MacArthur and Wayne Mack, and is now out of print. I was sitting on the campus of The Southern Baptist Theological Seminary when I read this article and was convinced of the fatal intellectual fallacies within the integration approach to Scripture and counseling. David Powlison's chapter, "The Sufficiency of Scripture to Diagnose and Cure Souls" was originally published in *The Journal of Biblical Counseling*. I read this article in my living room and was amazed at the profound and practical ability of Scripture to provide help for new and complex problems. Each one is crucial, and I am grateful to Wayne, Doug, and David—as well as to their publishers Christian Focus and CCEF—for permission to use these works in celebration of ACBC's 40th anniversary.

I pray that the Lord will use these articles in the lives of many people—as he used them in my life—to build up confidence in the Scriptures as we, the people of Christ, grow in the skill of caring for hurting people in a broken world.

Heath Lambert
August, 2016
Jacksonville, Florida

Chapter 1

What is Biblical Counseling?
Dr. Wayne Mack

The Chicago Statement on Biblical Inerrancy states that "the authority of scripture is a key issue for the Christian church in this and every age. Those who profess faith in Jesus Christ as Lord and Savior are called to show the reality of their discipleship by humbly and faithfully obeying God's written Word. To stray from Scripture in faith and conduct is disloyalty to our Master. Recognition of the total truth and trustworthiness of Holy Scripture is essential to a full grasp and adequate confession of its authority."

As a Christian, I wholeheartedly agree with every aspect of this general statement on biblical inerrancy and authority. I believe in both the inerrancy and authority of Holy Scripture. For me, the inerrancy and authority of Holy Scripture are like conjoined twins – they are inseparably joined to each other. Holy Scripture, being God's law and testimony, is true and should therefore serve as our standard for all matters of faith and practice (Isaiah 8:19-20; 2 Peter 1:3). God's Word being both truthful (John 17:17) and authoritative calls us to humble and faithful obedience in every area on which it speaks. There is no authority higher than the one found in Scripture. Wherever and on whatever subject the Scriptures speak, they must be regarded as both inerrant and authoritative.

As a Christian, it is because I affirm the preceding convictions that I believe in the sufficiency of Scripture in the area of counseling. Scripture is not silent about the matter of its sufficiency for both understanding man and his non-physical problems, and resolving those problems. To me, it is crystal clear about those issues. And because this is what I understand Scripture to be teaching about itself, my profession of faith in Jesus Christ as Lord and Savior compels me to submit to this sufficiency teaching. As I see it, doing anything else would amount to me being disloyal to my Master.

Today, many people affirm the inerrancy and authority of Scripture in matters of faith and practice, but do not affirm the sufficiency of Scripture for understanding and resolving the spiritual (non-physical) problems of man. They believe that we need the insights of psychology to understand and help people. In essence, they believe that when it comes to those matters, the Bible is fundamentally deficient. They believe that God did not design the Bible for this purpose, and consequently we must rely on extrabiblical psychological theories and insights. For many Christians, the Bible has a titular (given a title and respected in name) rather than a functional (actual, practical, real, respected in practice) authority in the area of counseling. It is acknowledged to be the Word of God and therefore worthy of our respect, but when it comes to understanding and resolving many of the real issues of life, it is considered to have limited value.

A Definition of Biblical Counseling

Biblical Counseling is Christ-Centered

The attitude that many Christians have toward Scripture was vividly illustrated by a person who visited to interview me about the kind of counseling I did. This person was traveling around the United States questioning various Christian counselors and asking them about their views on what constitutes Biblical counseling.[1] In the interview I said I believed that any counseling that was worthy of the name "Biblical" should be conscientiously and comprehensively Christ-centered. It will make much of who and what Christ is, and what He has done for us in His life, death, and resurrection. It will emphasize what He is doing for us right now in His intercession for us at the Father's right hand and what He will do for us in the future. It will also emphasize the Holy Spirit's present ministry in the believer's life. In biblical counseling, the Christ of the Bible is not to be an appendage. He is not a "tack on" for surviving life in the "fast lane." He needs to be at the core, as well as the circumference, our counseling. If we want to understand the nature and causes of a person's human difficulties, we need to understand the ways in which a person is unlike Christ in his or her values, aspirations, desires, thoughts, feelings, choices, attitudes, actions, and responses. Resolving a person's sin-related difficulties requires him to be redeemed and justified through Christ, receive God's forgiveness through Christ, and acquire from Christ enabling power to replace un-Christlike (sinful) patterns of life with Christlike (godly) ways of life.

In his book on Our Sufficiency in Christ, John MacArthur tells a story about a man who was shut out of a house on a cold night. He suffered some unpleasant consequences during the ordeal, all of which he could have avoided had he known he had, in his pocket, a key to the house. Dr MacArthur writes:

> That true story illustrates the predicament of Christians who try to gain access to God's blessings through human means, all the while possessing Christ, who is the key to

---

[1] Original term "Christian" has been changed to "biblical."

every spiritual blessing. He alone fulfills the deepest longing of our hearts and supplies every spiritual resource we need.

Believers have in Christ everything they will ever need to meet any trial, any craving, any difficulty they might ever encounter in this life. Even the newest convert possesses sufficient resources for every spiritual need. From the moment of salvation each believer is in Christ(2 Corinthians 5:17) and Christ is in the believer (Colossians 1:27). The Holy Spirit abides within as well (Romans 8:9) – the Christian is His temple (1 Corinthians 6:19). "Of His fullness we have all received, and grace upon grace" (John 1:16). So every Christian is a self-contained treasury of divinely bestowed spiritual affluence. There is nothing more – no great transcendental secret, no ecstatic experience, no hidden spiritual wisdom - that can take Christians to some higher plane of spiritual life. "His divine power has granted us everything pertaining to life and godliness, through the knowledge of Him who called us" (2 Peter 1:3, emphasis added). "The true knowledge of Him" refers to saving knowledge. To seek something more is like frantically knocking on a door, seeking what is inside, not realizing you hold the key in your pocket... No higher knowledge, no hidden truth, nothing besides the all-sufficient resources that we find in Christ exists that can change the human heart. Any counselor who desires to honor God and be effective must see the goal of his efforts as leading a person to the sufficiency of Christ. The view that man is capable of solving his own problems, or that people can help one another by "therapy" or other human means, denies the doctrine of human depravity and man's need for God. It replaces the Spirit's transforming power with impotent human wisdom.[2]

For Biblical counseling to take place, the people doing the counseling must be individuals who are conscientiously and comprehensively Christian in their outlook on life. Truly Biblical counseling is done by people who have experienced the regenerating work of the Holy Spirit, come to Christ in repentance and faith, acknowledged Him as Lord and Savior of their lives, and want to live in obedience to Him. Their main concern in life is to exalt Him and bring glory to His name. They believe that because God did not spare His own Son (from the cross) but delivered Him up (to the cross and death) for us (on our behalf as our substitute), He will freely give us – through Christ – all that we need for effective and productive living (for transforming us into the likeness of His Son). Truly Biblical counseling is done by those whose theological convictions influence, permeate, and control their personal lives and their counseling theory and practice.

---

[2] John MacArthur, Jr., *Our Sufficiency in Christ* (Dallas: Word Publishing, 1991), pp. 27, 72. In the last paragraph quoted, MacArthur is referring to attempts to help people based on secular humanistic theories, techniques, and therapies. He is not referring to the kind of counseling being described in this chapter, as is evidenced from many of his other writings and his co-authored book entitled Introduction to Biblical Counseling, as well as the facts that the church he pastors has a very active counselor training program and counseling ministry, and that the Master's College, of which he is president, has an undergraduate major in biblical counseling and a graduate program leading to an M.A. in biblical counseling.

Biblical Counseling Is Church-Centered

Another major distinctive of truly Biblical counseling that I mentioned to my interviewer was that it is conscientiously and comprehensively church-centered. The Scriptures clearly teach that the local church is the primary means by which God intends to accomplish His work in the world. The local church is His ordained instrument for calling the lost to Himself. It is also the context in which He sanctifies and changes His people into the likeness of Christ. According to Scripture, the church is His household, the pillar and ground of the truth (1 Timothy 3:15), and the instrument He uses to help His people put off the old manner of life (pre-Christian ways of thinking, feeling choosing, and acting) and put on the new self (a new manner of life with Christlike thoughts, feelings, choices, actions, values, and responses – Ephesians 4:1-32). Even a cursory reading of the New Testament will lead a person to the conclusion that the church is at the center of God's program for His people. Jesus Christ, who proclaimed that He would build His church (Matthew 16:18), invested in it authority to act with the imprimatur of heaven (Matthew 18:17-20) and ultimately revealed that His plan was to fill the world with local bodies of believers (Matthew 28:18-20).

When trying to capture and project his conception of the role of the church in God's program and with God's people, John Calvin made this impassioned assertion:

> Because it is now our intention to discuss the visible church, let us learn from the simple title "mother" how useful, indeed necessary, it is that we should know her. For there is no other way to enter life unless this mother conceive us in her womb, give us birth, nourish us at her breast, and lastly, unless she keep us under her care and guidance until,

putting off mortal flesh, we become like the angels (Matthew 22:30). Our weakness does not allow us to be dismissed from her school until we have been pupils all our lives...God's fatherly favor and the especial witness of spiritual life are limited to his flock, so that it is always disastrous to leave the church.[3]

This statement about the church by John Calvin was not specifically directed toward the issue of counseling, but it does indicate Calvin's perspective on the importance of the church in the lives of believers. His view concurs with the ideas that the church is responsible for providing counseling and Christians are responsible for seeking care and guidance in their personal lives. Calvin's study of the Scriptures convinced him that the nurture, edification, and sanctification of believers was to be church-centered. I wholeheartedly agree with this emphasis because I believe that is the unmistakable teaching of Holy Scripture.[4]

Biblical Counseling Is Bible-Based

As I continued to explain my views on Christian counseling, I told my visitor that truly Christian counseling is *conscientiously and comprehensively Bible-based*, deriving from the Bible an understanding of who man is, the nature of his main problems, why he has these problems, and how to resolve them. For counseling to be worthy of the name of Christ, the counselor must

---

[3] John Calvin, *Institutes of the Christian Religion*, 2:1012.

[4] More about the role of the church in the lives of believers may be found in the book *Life in the Father's House: A Member's Guide to the Local Church*, Wayne Mack and David Swavely (Phillipsburg, NJ: Presbyterian & Reformed, 1996).

be conscientiously and comprehensively committed to the *sufficiency of Scripture* for understanding and resolving all of the non-physical personal and interpersonal sin-related difficulties of man.

Questioning the Sufficiency of Scripture

At this point, the individual who had come to ask about my views on Christian counseling responded by saying, "Well, what you're saying about all of these things is nice, but what do you think should be done when people have really serious problems?" Now, consider what this person – who claimed to be a Christian – was implying by asking that question. She was implying that the factors I had mentioned might prove to be helpful for people who have minor problems, but certainly they are not enough for resolving the really serious problems of life. She was intimating that the approach I had described was rather simplistic. She was suggesting that the resources that God prescribes in His Word for ministering to needy people are not adequate. She was insinuating that the substantial insights necessary for ministering to people with major difficulties must be gleaned from sources other than the ones I had mentioned.[5]

The Shortcomings of Extrabiblical Insights

There are three reasons why I reject the idea that Biblical counselors need extrabiblical insights to do truly effective counseling.

---

[5] In the original draft, Dr. Mack quotes and argues from a section of Doug Bookman's chapter "The Word of God and Counseling" which is the next chapter in this publication.

Limitations of Human Knowledge

The first reason is related to the finiteness of man's knowledge. The fact that man is finite necessarily limits the extent and validity of his knowledge. Even Adam, the first man, was a finite human being who needed God's revelation to rightly understand God, himself, what was right and wrong, what was true and what was false, what should be believed and what should not be believed (Genesis 1:26-28; 2:15-17, 24). An old fable about six blind men who all bumped into and felt different parts of the same elephant illustrates the futility of man's attempts to find absolute truth by the usual means of intuition, reason or logic, or empirical research. As the story goes, one approached the elephant from the front and grasped his trunk and said, "An elephant is like a fire hose." The second blind man happened to touch one of the animal's tusks and said, "An elephant is like a thick spear." The third blind man felt the elephant's side and said, "An elephant is like a wall." The fourth blind man, who approached the elephant from the rear and gripped its tail, said, "An elephant is like a rope." The fifth blind man grabbed hold of one of the elephant's legs and said, "An elephant is like the trunk of a tree." The sixth man, who was tall, grabbed one of the elephant's ears and said, "An elephant is like a fan."

Which of these depictions of an elephant was correct? None of them! And why? Because each blind man encountered or experienced only a limited portion of the whole elephant. Their knowledge of what an elephant was like was restricted and even erroneous because of the limitations of their experience and perception. And so it is and always must be with finite mortal man when it comes to the matter of discerning absolute truth apart from revelation from the living God, who knows all things and sees the whole picture clearly and perfectly. A recent newspaper article reminded me of the futility of thinking that finite man can discover absolute truth apart from divine revelation. In this tongue-in-cheek article entitled "Education's Duplicity, Uselessness," Russell Baker writes:

> Pluto may not be a planet. Can you believe it? Is everything we learn in school a lie?
> This Pluto business is the last straw in the duplicity and uselessness of education. Now I have to deal with Plutonic revisionism, and I haven't even recovered from the discovery that you should not eat a good breakfast.
> "Always eat a good breakfast." That's what they taught us in school. They said it was good for us.
> Well, you know it, I know it, we all know it: they were wrong. We now know a good breakfast is bad for you. Those eggs sunny side up, that crisp bacon, the buttersoaked toast covered with jelly – bad for you.
> So now we always eat a bad breakfast because they say a bad breakfast is good for you.
> And remember the milk? Remember paying the milk money and having milk served right there in the classroom? What kind of milk was it?
> Was it skim milk? Was it low-fat milk? Ha! You know it wasn't. It was milk with all the evil left in.
> And they said it was good for you. Good for you! It was clogging your arteries and hastening your trip to the grave. And they called that an education!
> The older you get the clearer it becomes that education for the young may not only be useless, but downright dangerous.[6]

[6] Russell Baker, *Education's Duplicity, Uselessness*, The New York Times,

At this point in the article, Baker goes on to make a few more tongue-in-cheek remarks about the way what we once considered to be truth has been revised. After having done this, he concludes with these words:

> Many people become as irked as I do about the incessant need to keep up with today's wisdom by abandoning or revising yesterday's. And of course today's wisdom will just as inevitably have to be abandoned or revised as the future bears down upon us.
> You can bet the world has not faced the last revision of knowledge about Pluto, or about what constitutes a good breakfast. The revising of what we think of as knowledge goes on forever, and always has.
> The truth about knowledge seems to be that its truth is only a sometimes thing, that what we accept as truth this year will have to be abandoned as the world turns. This endless abandonment and revision is usually said to result from progress. But suppose progress is also an idea doomed to be abandoned. What if there is no such thing as progress, but only change?[7]

In his article, Baker astutely identifies the tentative nature of our humanly discovered knowledge or "truth" as he asserts that "what we accept as truth this year will have to be abandoned or revised." And why is humanly discovered "truth... only a sometimes thing"? One reason is because man's finiteness necessarily limits the extent and validity of his knowledge.

March 16, 1996.

[7] ibid.

Depravity of Human Nature

A second factor that causes me to reject the idea that Christian counselors should welcome and depend on extrabiblical insights and therapies is connected to the biblical teaching about the depravity of man's nature since the Fall of Adam in Genesis 3. Any biblical discussion of how man comes to know truth must include a consideration of what theologians often refer to as the "noetic"[8] effects of sin. Scripture clearly teaches that every aspect of man's being has been affected by sin. Man's character, speech, and behavior have all been perverted by sin[9] – as well as his emotions and desires, his conscience and will, his intellect, his thought processes, his goals and motives, and the way he views and interprets life. None of man's faculties have escaped the corrupting, corrosive, perverting, and debilitating impact of sin. In reference to the cognitive, motivational, and emotional aspects of man's being, Scripture asserts that:

> The heart is more deceitful than all else and is desperately sick; who can understand it? (Jeremiah 17:9).

> God has looked down from heaven upon the sons of men, to see if there is anyone who understands (Psalm 53:2).

---

[8] The word noetic is related to the Greek word nous, which is translated by the English word mind. This word denotes "the seat of reflection, consciousness, comprising the faculties of perception and understanding, and those of feeling, judging, and determining," as defined in W.E. Vine, An Expository Dictionary of New Testament Words (Westwood: Revell, 1957), p. 69.

[9] See Romans 1:18–2:23; 1 Kings 8:46; Psalm 51:5; 58:3; Isaiah 53:6; 64:6; Psalm14:1-7; Ephesians 2:1-3; Romans 8:8.

The wrath of God is revealed from heaven against all ungodliness and unrighteousness of men, who suppress the truth in unrighteousness... Professing to be wise, they became fools... For they exchanged the truth of God for a lie, and worshiped and served the creature rather than the Creator, who is blessed forever... And just as they did not see fit to acknowledge God any longer, God gave them over to a depraved mind (Romans 1:18, 22, 25, 28).

The mind set on the flesh is hostile toward God (Romans 8:7).

You were formerly alienated and hostile in mind (Colossians 1:21).

To the pure, all things are pure; but to those who are defiled and unbelieving, nothing is pure, but both their mind and their conscience are defiled (Titus 1:15).

Out of the heart come evil thoughts (Matthew 15:19).

In commenting on the noetic effects of sin, Edward Reynolds wrote:

Look into the mind; you shall find it full of vanity, wasting and wearying itself in childishness, impertinent, unprofitable notions, "full of ignorance and darkness," no man knoweth, nay no man hath so much acknowledged, as to enquire or seek after God in the way whereby he will be found. *Nay more, when God breaks in upon the mind, by some notable testimony from his creatures, judgments, or providence – yet they like it not, they hold it down, they reduce themselves back again to foolish hearts, to reprobate and undiscerning minds, as naturally as hot water returns to its former coldness.* Full of curiosity, rash, unprofitable enquiries, foolish and unlearned questions, profane babblings...perverse disputes, all the fruits of corrupt and rotten minds. Full of pride and contradiction against the truth, "oppositions of science," that is, setting up of philosophy and vain deceits, imaginations, thoughts, fleshly reasonings against the spirit and truth which is in Jesus. Full of... fleshly wisdom, human inventions... of rules and methods of its own to... come to happiness. Full of inconstancy and roving swarms of empty and foolish thoughts, slipperiness, and unstableness... (emphasis added).[10]

What a clear description of sin's effects on the mind of man! "But," you may ask, "what does this teaching about the noetic effect of sin have to do with whether or not Christian counselors should accept and use extrabiblical insights in their counseling efforts?"

The answer to that question is simple: Scripture teaches that the minds of unredeemed men have been adversely affected by sin and, as a result, even if they observe something accurately, they are likely to interpret it wrongly. Because they have the kind of mind (including all the cognitive, motivational, and emotional aspects previously mentioned) described in the preceding Bible verses, unregenerate – and even to some extent, regenerate – men will tend to distort truth. The only way we can think rightly is to allow the Holy Spirit to renew our minds so that we will learn to

---

[10] Edward Reynolds, *The Sinfulness of Sin* (Ligonfer, PA: Sola Deo Gloria, 1992 reprint of 1826 ed.), p. 123.

look at, interpret, and understand life through the lens of Scripture (Psalm 36:9; 119:104; Isaiah 8:19-20; Romans 1:18-32; 12:2; Ephesians 4:23).

When he commented on the role that secular disciplines should play in biblical counseling, David Powlison vividly described the noetic impact of sin on man's thinking processes:

> Secular disciplines may serve us well as they describe people; they may challenge us by how they seek to explain, guide, and change people; but they seriously mislead us when we take them at face value because they are secular. They explain people, define what people ought to be like, and try to solve people's problems without considering God and man's relationship to God. Secular disciplines have made a systematic commitment to being wrong.
> This is not to deny that secular people are often brilliant observers of other human beings. They are often ingenious critics and theoreticians. But they also distort what they see and mislead by what they teach and do, because from God's point of view the wisdom of the world has fundamental folly written through it. They will not acknowledge that God has created human beings as God-related and God-accountable creatures. The mind-set of secularity is like a power saw with a set that deviates from the right angle. It may be a powerful saw, and it may cut a lot of wood, but every board comes out crooked.[11]

Because of our finiteness and sinfulness, our understanding of man and his problems can be trusted only when our thoughts and

---

[11] David Powlison, in *Introduction to Biblical Counseling*, pp. 365-66.

insights reflect the teaching of Holy Scripture. We simply are not able to ascertain truth apart from divine revelation. In another work, I wrote:

> We have no standard by which we can evaluate whether something is true or false except the Word of God. Thus while we can be confident that whatever we share with our counselees from the Word of God is true, we should have a healthy skepticism about any theory or insight that does not proceed from Scripture. If it is not taught by the Word of God alone, it may be error.[12]

In his book *Every Thought Captive*, Richard Pratt explains man's epistemological predicament apart from divine relation this way:

> All that can properly be called truth, not just "religious truth," resides first in God and men know truly only as they come to God's revelation of Himself as the source of truth... (Psalm 94:10)... This dependence on God in the area of knowledge does not mean that men are without the true ability to think and reason... Men do actually think, yet true knowledge is dependent on and derived from God's knowledge as it has been revealed to man.[13]

"But," someone may ask, "what about those statements that finite and sinful men make that seem to be a reiteration of concepts and ideas taught by Scripture? Must we regard these observations as

---

[12] Wayne Mack, in *Introduction to Biblical Counseling*, p.254.

[13] Richard Pratt, *Every Thought Captive* (Phillipsburg, NJ: Presbyterian & Reformed, 1979), p. 17.

false because people did not get them from the Bible?" These questions may be answered in these ways:

1. People may have been influenced by biblical teaching through various means and not even be aware of it, nor give the Bible credit for their insights. But even if this occurs, they will always distort scriptural teaching and put their own spin on it. They may, for example, talk about the importance of God, prayer, forgiveness, dealing with guilt, taking responsibility, love, confession, or the spiritual dimension in life. On the surface, a person's teaching on these concepts may seem biblical, but upon further investigation the theologically, biblically trained person will discover that not everything that sounds the same is the same. People may be using the same words or presenting the same concepts that God mentions in His Word, but they may also be filling those words and concepts with completely different meanings. In fact, the Bible tells us that men will suppress, deny, and distort the truth even if it is staring them in the face (Romans 1:18; 1 Corinthians 2:14).

2. Extrabiblical statements that seem to reflect biblical truth must be regarded as false because, as Richard Pratt states, "they are not the result of voluntary obedience to God's revelation."[14]

3. "Beyond this," Pratt continues, "the statements are falsified by the non-Christian framework of meaning and therefore lead away from the worship of God. If nothing else, the

---

[11] ibid.

mere commitment to human independence falsifies the non-Christian's statements."[15]

The Sufficiency of Scripture

My third reason for rejecting the idea that Christian counselors need extrabiblical insights is that the Bible says God has given us – in our union with Christ and in His Word – everything that is necessary for living and for godliness (2 Peter 1:3). Scripture clearly says that it contains all the principles and practical insights that are necessary for understanding people and their problems (as we'll see in a moment). So apart from the question of whether it is possible to integrate the ideas of man with the truths of God's Word is the issue of whether or not it is necessary. On this matter, I am convinced the Scripture's own testimony about its sufficiency, adequacy, and superiority is abundantly plain.

To demonstrate this I could cite numerous passages of Scripture, but for the sake of time and space I will refer to only three representative passages: one from the Old Testament and two from the New. Psalm 19:7-11 makes numerous statements about the Bible that no one would ever consider making about the ideas of any man. In this text, assertions are made that set the Bible in a class all by itself – statements that unmistakably demonstrate the Bible's sufficiency and superiority over any of man's theories. Consider carefully what this passage says about what Scripture is and what it can do, and then think of the counseling implications of these assertions. According to Psalm 19:7-11, Scripture:

---

[15] ibid.

1.   Is *perfect* (whole, complete, sufficient, lacking nothing) and therefore able to restore (transform, renew, restore) the soul (the inner man, the real self) – verse 7.

2.   Is a *sure* (trustworthy, reliable, dependable) witness and therefore able to make wise the simple (people who lack a proper understanding of life, God, themselves, others) – verse 7.

3.   Contains precepts (principles, guidelines, rules for character and conduct) that are *right* (correct, in accord with what is just and good, appropriate and fitting) and therefore able to cause the heart (the totality of man's inner non-physical self) to rejoice (to experience a sense of well-being, serenity, tranquility, and peace) – verse 8.

4.   Is *authoritative* (it gives mandates and directives that are always correct) and pure (clear, untainted with evil or error) and therefore able to bring light into man's chaos and confusion, to replace man's ignorance and lack of understanding with clear direction, perspective, and insight – verse 8.

5.   Is *clean* (uncontaminated, free from impurity, defilement) and enduring (permanent, unchanging, relevant, up to date, never outdated, never in need of alteration) and therefore able to produce the fear of the Lord (a wholesome and incredibly practical and positive reverence for God) – verse 9.

6.   *Provides insights* about God, man, life, and everything needed for living and godliness that are altogether true (they

correspond to and accurately reflect reality, they tell it like it really is) and righteous (they reflect that which is right, good, and holy, that which is truly just and fair) and therefore lead men to understand and practice what is truly real and right –verse 9.

7. Being "more desirable than gold, yes, than much fine gold," is able to produce in us a kind of *prosperity* that is more valuable than all the material riches of the world – verse 10.

8. Being "sweeter also than honey and the drippings of the honeycomb," is able to remove the sourness, acidity, and bitterness caused by sin and to produce in us a *sweetness* of life that surpasses anything the world can provide – verse 10.

9. Possessing all of the previously noted qualities, is able to infallibly *warn and protect* us from the many dangers and disasters that can result from an ignorance of what is truly right – verse 11.

10. Possessing all of the previously noted characteristics, is able to *preserve* us from temptation, sin, error, false teaching, and every other threat to the health and well-being of our inner man - our thoughts, emotions, affections, and attitudes – verse 11.

Believing as I do in the inspiration, inerrancy, and authority of the Scriptures, Psalm 19:7-11 settles the sufficiency issue for me. If words mean anything, how could I come to any other conclusion? But there's more – much more. And some of that

29

"more" is found in 2 Timothy 3:1-17. In the thirteen verses of this chapter, Paul delineates a host of problems representative of what counselors often encounter in their attempts to help people. Many people who require counseling do so because they are struggling with difficulties that stem from one or more of the sinful attitudes, desires, and actions that Paul mentions in this rich passage.

Some people seek counseling because of problems that are associated with being "lovers of self, lovers of money, boastful, arrogant, revilers, disobedient to parents, ungrateful, unholy, unloving, irreconcilable, malicious gossips, without self-control, brutal, haters of good, treacherous, reckless, conceited, lovers of pleasure rather than lovers of God" (verses 2-4). Some individuals need counseling because they are "holding to a form of godliness, although they have denied its power" (verse 5). Some are struggling because they are "weighed down with sins, led on by various impulses" (verse 6). Many experience severe difficulties in their lives that are related to pride, opposition to and rebellion against God's truth, ungodly thoughts, deceitful patterns of living, and relating to people. Unpleasant, distressing difficulties that motivate people to seek counseling occur because they are "always learning and never able to come to the truth" or because they live in the midst of a society of people who are vile and hypocritical – people who are going "from bad to worse" (2 Timothy 3:6-13). People need counseling either because they are personally experiencing and manifesting sinful attitudes, desires, and behaviors; or they are personally suffering from the influence of people who manifest the sinful patterns depicted in this passage.

Where do we turn for resources to minister to these kinds of people? What do we need for understanding and resolving their problems? Paul answers that question in verses 14-17. At this point in his epistle, he turns from a description of the kinds of problems that people experience in this sin-cursed world to a description of the resources Christians have for ministering to the people he has just described in the first thirteen verses. In clear and unmistakable words, Paul tells us that the resources we need for ministering to people who live in a 2 Timothy 3:1-13 society are found in Scripture. In concise, direct terms, Paul extols the Bible's total adequacy for ministering to people whose lives are characterized or affected by the things mentioned in verses 1-13.

Why is Scripture Adequate?

According to Paul, the Scripture is totally adequate because:

1. *It is holy or sacred* (verse 15). It is set apart from any other writing or literary production; it is unique; it is in a class all by itself. No other writing can compare with what is written in the Scriptures.

2. *It is able* (verse 15). It has power to do things to and in people. "It is," as Jay Adams has written, "the Holy Spirit's tool for working in the minds and hearts of men and women to make them like Christ. Being peculiarly associated with the Spirit both in its composition and in its use, the Bible is powerful, able to transform lives."[16]

3. *It is inspired by God* (verse 16). Literally, the Greek word translated "inspired" means "God breathed." So Paul is telling us that the Bible is unique and able because its truths had their origin in God; they are not merely some man's

---

[16] Jay Adams, *How to Help People Change* (Grand Rapids, MI: Zondervan, 1986), pp. 23-24.

opinions or discoveries or insights. As Peter said, "no prophecy of Scripture is a matter of one's own interpretation, for no prophecy was ever made by an act of human will, but men moved by the Holy Spirit spoke from God" (2 Peter 1:20-21). That is why, when quoting a portion of Psalm 2 (a psalm written by David), the early Christians said that the truth found in this psalm came to us from God by the Holy Spirit through the mouth of David (Acts 4:24-26). To the early Christians, the words of Scripture were authoritative and sufficient because, even though they came through the agency of holy men, they ultimately had their origin in God.

4. *It is profitable or useful* (verse 16). God's Word has utilitarian value; it enhances life; it is profitable in every way – for time and eternity, for our relationships with God and our fellow man, for our spiritual and emotional and mental well-being, for our marriages and families, for our goals and motivations, for guidance and direction, for comfort and challenge, for preventing and resolving our inner and interpersonal problems, for all of life. It is useful for teaching; it is the instrument the Holy Spirit uses to provide for us a standard of what is right and wrong, good and bad, true and false about all the truly important matters of life. Scripture is useful for reproof; the Holy Spirit uses it to convict us of sin and show us when we are wrong in our thinking, motives, desires, attitudes, feelings, values, and reactions. It is the instrument the Holy Spirit uses to bring us under conviction and motivate us to want to repent and change.

    God's Word is also useful for correction; the Holy Spirit uses it to point us in the right direction and correct our sinful thoughts, motives, feelings, actions, and speech. It not only shows us what we need to change, but also tells us how to change and what to change to. And Scripture is profitable for training; it is the instrument the Holy Spirit uses to help us to develop new patterns of life. Scripture makes that which is unnatural - living righteously - natural; and makes that which is difficult – living God's way – easier. It helps us to develop strength in the areas in which we are weak.

5. *It can thoroughly equip the man of God for every good work* (verse 17). Through Scripture, the Holy Spirit thoroughly equips His servants – people of God – to do everything He wants them to do in the kind of society described in 2 Timothy 3:1-13. Do God's people need anything more than Scripture to effectively minister to the people living in the world described in verses 1-13? Is anything else really necessary? Absolutely not! Through Scripture, every believer can be thoroughly equipped. In Scripture, Christians have everything they need to understand people and their problems and to help them resolve those problems.[17]

John Murray draws the following conclusion about 2 Timothy3:15-17: "There is no situation in which we (as men of God) are placed, no demand that arises for which Scripture as the deposit of the manifold wisdom of God is not adequate and sufficient".[18]

---

[17] See Adams' book *How to Help People Change* for a fuller explanation and application of 2 Timothy 3:14-17.

[18] John Murray, *Collected Writings* (London: Banner of Truth, 1975), 3:261.

Our Sufficiency in Christ

Perhaps there is no better summary of the Bible's teaching about our complete sufficiency in Christ than the one given by the apostle Peter when he wrote that by His divine power, God "has granted to us everything pertaining to life and godliness" (2 Peter 1:3). "Life" has to do with everything related to living effectively and biblically in our daily activities and relationships with our environment and other people. "Godliness" has to do with our relationship with God – with living a God-centered, Godconscious life marked by godly character and conduct.

In 2 Peter 1:4-8, Peter defines "everything pertaining to life and godliness" as "*becoming partakers of the divine nature* " (emphasis added). It involves being born again or from above; becoming a new creation in Christ Jesus; receiving from God a new nature with new dispositions, desires, interests, potential, and power; putting on the new self; and being renewed in the image of God (Romans 6:1-11; 2 Corinthians 5:17; Colossians 3:10; 1 Peter 1:23; 2 Peter 1:4; 1 John 3:1-18). It involves the capacity to "escape the corruption in the world caused by evil desires" (2 Peter 1:4 NIV). It involves developing the qualities of faith, moral excellence, true knowledge, self-control, perseverance, godliness, brotherly kindness, and Christian love (2 Peter 1:4-7) so that you might live a useful life for Christ (verses 8-10). Life and godliness also involves being able to deal successfully with the issues that are present in the lives of people who seek counseling. People who are in need of counseling lack the qualities Peter mentions in 2 Peter 1:4-7 and need help in developing them. It's interesting to observe that people whose lives do reflect these qualities don't need much formal counseling. This passage, then, is pregnant with counseling implications.

Notice that Peter said that God has, by His divine power, "granted to us everything pertaining to life and godliness" (2 Peter 1:3, emphasis added). Everything that is needed to develop this kind of life and acquire the qualities in verses 4-7 has been granted to us by God. And how do we tap into these powerful, all sufficient resources? Peter declared that these divine resources become ours through the true knowledge of God and of Jesus our Lord, and through the medium of His precious and magnificent promises (2 Peter 1:2-4). In other words, the repository of the everything we need for life and godliness is found in our glorious and excellent God and His precious and magnificent Word.

Our sufficiency as Christians is found in a deeper, fuller, lifechanging knowledge of the glory and excellence of God and the magnificence and preciousness of His promises. Michael Green observed that God has called us to share "something of His moral excellence in this life, and of His glory hereafter... The triple agency of the promises, the power and the Person of the Lord regenerate a man and make him a sharer in God's own nature, so that the family likeness begins to be seen in him."[19]

Worthy of Full Confidence

In the light of what we've learned from Psalm 19:7-11, 2 Timothy 3:15-17, and 2 Peter 1:3-7 I ask this question: Could God have stated more clearly the sufficiency of our resources in Christ and in His Word? What more could He have said to get the message through to us that we do not need any extrabiblical resources to understand people and their problems and help them

---

[19] Michael Green, *Second Epistle of Peter and the Epistle of Jude* (Grand Rapids, MI: Eerdmans, 1968), p. 64.

develop the qualities, attitudes, desires, values, feelings, and behavior that are proper for relating to and living before God in a way that pleases and honors Him?

A consideration of the truths presented in those three passages and many other sections of Scripture forces me to draw three conclusions:

1.   The inerrant Bible to which Christians are committed as an authority in life teaches that God has provided for us in His Word whatever is true and necessary for successful living. It declares that God has given us, in the Bible, everything we need for living in right relationship with God, ourselves, and other people.

2.   Because that is true, professing Christians have two options: either they must yield to the Bible's teaching on this matter or they must abandon the idea that the Bible is inerrant and authoritative. It is either inerrant and authoritative and also sufficient, or it is none of those things. If the Bible claims to be sufficient and it isn't, then you cannot say it is inerrant and authoritative. Given what the Bible teaches about itself, you simply cannot have it both ways.

3.   This final conclusion is a natural concomitant of accepting the truthfulness of the first conclusion: because the Bible asserts its own sufficiency for counseling-related issues, secular psychology has nothing to offer for understanding or providing solutions to the non-physical problems of people. When it comes to counseling people, we have no reason to depend on the insights of finite and fallen men. Rather, we have every reason to place our confidence in the sure, dependable, and entirely trustworthy revelation of

God given to us in Holy Scripture because it contains a God-ordained, sufficient, comprehensive system of theoretical commitments, principles, insights, goals, and appropriate methods for understanding and resolving the non-physical problems of people. It provides for us a model that needs no supplement. God, the expert on helping people, has given us in Scripture counseling perspectives and methodology that are wholly adequate for resolving our sin-related problems.

The Need for Caution

David Powlison has stated well the danger of including extrabiblical ideas in the counsel offered to or by Christians:

Let us clarify first what we mean by counseling methodology. A counseling methodology is a system of theoretical commitments, principles, goals, and appropriate methods. It is a set of interconnected things; it is not a collection or random and eclectic bits of observation or technique. A counseling methodology is an organized, committed way of understanding and tackling people's problems.
Do secular disciplines have anything to offer to the methodology of biblical counseling? The answer is a flat no. Scriptures provide the system for Biblical counseling. Other disciplines – history, anthro-pology, literature, sociology, psychology, biology, business, political science – may be useful in a variety of secondary ways to the pastor and the biblical counselor, but such disciplines can never provide a system for understanding and counseling people.

God is the expert when it comes to people, and He has spoken and acted to change us and equip us to help others change.[20]

Secular psychology may play an *illustrative* (providing examples and details that, when carefully and radically reinterpreted, illustrate the biblical model) or *provocative* (challenging us to study the Scriptures more thoroughly to develop our model in areas we have not thought about or have neglected or misconstrued) function, but, because of man's finiteness and fallenness, the insights, methodologies, and practices of secular psychology are in many instances dangerously unbiblical, dishonoring to God, and harmful to people. Other aspects of secular psychology are at best neutral and therefore unnecessary.

None of the illustrations, observations, or details that secularists present are necessary for the task of understanding and helping people. We already have all we need – the authoritative, indispensable, perspicuous, sufficient, and superior revelation of God in His Word (Isaiah 8:19-20). Why, then, would any Christian think that we must turn to extrabiblical theories or the practices of men for understanding and promoting change in people?

Bible-Based Resources for Man's Problems

Because the purpose of this chapter was to demonstrate that the Bible asserts its sufficiency for understanding and resolving the kinds of issues that counselors (Christian or non-Christian) deal with in their attempts to help people, I have not taken time to provide specific examples of how the Scriptures actually do help us or to provide details about a biblical methodology for counseling.

---

[20] David Powlison, in *Introduction to Biblical Counseling*, p.365.

Should you desire to pursue "the how to" more fully, I have listed some recommended resources.[21] In these resources, you will find information about a biblical counseling methodology for understanding and resolving the problems of people. You will find case studies and teaching that illustrates the sufficiency of Scripture

---

[21] In *Introduction to Biblical Counseling*, eds. MacArthur and Mack, chapters 10-16, 20. Wayne Mack has developed many books and audio and video-tapes of counseling courses, including tapes dealing with a biblical approach to counseling on a variety of specific issues (a catalog listing these materials is available by writing to him at 21726 W. Placerita Canyon Rd., Santa Clarita, CA 91322); Christian Counseling and Educational Foundation West has videotapes of several counseling courses, and they offer many training courses (3495 College Avenue, San Diego, CA 92115); Christian Counseling and Educational Foundation East offers courses on biblical counseling and produces an excellent journal – The Biblical Counseling Journal – for biblical counselors (1803 East Willow Grove Ave., Laverock, PA 19118); the National Association of Nouthetic Counselors (NANC) sponsors conferences, produces a biblical counseling publication, and has audio and videotapes on numerous "how to" issues (NANC, 5526, State Road 26 East, Lafayette, IN 47905); Jay Adams has written numerous books and produced many audio and videotapes on various biblical counseling issues (Woodruff, SC: Timeless Texts); Gary Almy, Addicted to Recovery (Eugene, OR: Harvest House); Ed Bulkley, Only God Can Heal the Wounded Heart (Eugene, OR: Harvest House); David Powlison, Power Encounters (Grand Rapids, MI: Baker Book House); Edward Welch, Counselor's Guide to the Brain and Its Disorder: Knowing the Difference Between Sin and Disease (Grand Rapids, MI: Zondervan); William Playfair, The Useful Lie (Wheaton, IL: Crossway Books); D. Martyn Lloyd-Jones, Spiritual Depression: Its Causes and Its Cure (Grand Rapids, MI: Eerdmans); Michael Bobick, From Slavery to Sonship: A Biblical Psychology for Pastoral Counseling (available from Grace Book Shack, 13248 Roscoe Blvd., Sun Valley, CA 91352); Sound Word Cassettes carries many audio and videotapes on counseling various problems biblically (430 Boyd Circle, P.O. Box 2035, Mail Station, Michigan City, IN 46330); Westminster Theological Seminary (Chestnut Hill, P.O. Box 27009, Philadelphia, PA 19118, and 1725 Bear Valley Parkway, Escondido CA 92027) offers many counseling courses that provide a biblical approach on various counseling issues; degree programs are available in biblical counseling at Trinity College and Theological Seminary, 4233 Medwel Dr., Box 717, Newburgh, IN 47629-0171.

for people who claim to be suffering from multiple personality disorder (MPD); various kinds of eating disorders; sexual sins such as incest, homosexuality, transvestism, transsexualism, slavery to pornography and lust; depression; anxiety; anger; bizarre, schizophrenic behavior; drug abuse, including alcoholism; and what secularists would call obsessive, compulsive disorders. You will find biblically based information about problems of the past, self-esteem problems, chronic fatigue, demon possession, chemical imbalance, victimization, suffering human defensiveness, women in menopause, women and PMS, confidentiality in counseling, crisis counseling, guilt, panic attacks, inordinate fears, psychological testing, ADHD, rebuilding a marriage after adultery, counseling various kinds of marriage and family problems, and other counseling issues.

Chapter 2

The Word of God and Counseling
Dr. Doug Bookman

Epistemology is defined as "an inquiry into the nature and source of knowledge, the bounds of knowledge, and the justification of claims to knowledge."[22] It is the final element of that definition which is at stake here, the investigation into the broad and foundational question: "How do we *know* that what we *think* we know is in fact *true*?"

Any Christian who sets out to counsel another individual must certainly be gripped by the reality that the counsel he offers must be *true*. Counseling is by definition and impulse a helping ministry. It assumes one individual who is confronted with some measure of confusion, disappointment, or despair and a second person who endeavors to help by analyzing the counselee's situation, sorting out the issues involved, and then offering helpful and healing advice and direction. But the efficacy of all that any counselor undertakes to do is dependent at least on this one thing: that his analysis and counsel is *true*. Thus, any thoughtful consideration of the ministry of counseling must begin with the most basic of all philosophical questions, that question articulated by a Roman prefect 2000 years ago, "What is truth?"

Ever since its genesis as a distinguishable discipline almost four decades ago, the school of thought and ministry broadly known as Christian Psychology has been convulsed by the issue of its own epistemological construct. (That is, where ought/may Christians go to find the *truth* necessary to help people who are hurting?) Because that discipline grew up largely within the broad

---

[22] Paul Feinberg, *Epistemology*, in *The Evangelical Dictionary of Theology* (Grand Rapids, MI: Baker, 1984), p 359.

limits of evangelical Christianity, there has been the universal acknowledgement of the veracity of the answer offered by the One to whom the Roman prefect posed that question so long ago, the answer articulated by Jesus when, as He addressed His Heavenly Father in prayer, He stated simply, "Thy Word is truth."

But for most that answer alone has not sufficed. There has been the persuasion – articulated, justified, and applied in various ways – that there is *truth* which is at least *profitable* and perhaps even *necessary* to the effort to help by means of counseling, and which is to be discovered *beyond the pages of Scripture.* Christians thus persuaded are anxious to affirm Jesus' simple but profound declaration that the Word of God is truth, but they feel compelled to qualify that affirmation with the proposition that those Scriptural truths may (or even must) be supplemented by truths which are not recorded in the pages of Scripture but which have been discovered by human investigation and observation. This persuasion lies at the very heart of the integrationist impulse of Christian Psychology.[23]

---

[23] The term "integration," used to denote the effort to define the relationship between theology and psychology and the limits to which the two may\may not be understood in concert with one another, is not entirely satisfactory, but it has certainly become the term of choice in virtually every discussion of that issue. Fleck and Carter [*Psychology and Christianity: Integrative Readings*, (Nashville: Abingdon, 1981), J. Roland Fleck and John D. Carter, eds., p 16] discuss the implications and delimitations of the term carefully, acknowledging that it is rather arbitrary and can be misunderstood, that there have been attempts to displace the term (with words such as "synthesis" or "psychotheology"), but that with proper qualifications it is the term that serves the most effectively and is employed almost universally. Compare J. Harold Ellens rather acerbic critique of the term in "Biblical Themes in Psychological Theory and Practice," *CAPS* [1980:6(2) p 2].

By all accounts, this integrationist tendency is rather recent in origin.[24] Throughout much of the twentieth century a spirit of mutual mistrust and even contempt existed between the worlds of secular psychology and Christian theology. But that hostility began to thaw in certain circles sometime in the mid-part of the 20th century,[25] and by the last decade of that century there existed a manifest spirit of reconciliation between Christianity and psychology in many quarters. Indeed, many devotees of Christian psychology evidence a greater measure of fraternity with the secular psychological community than with those Christians who are compelled by their theology to reject entirely the discipline of secular psychotherapy.[26]

---

[24] Fleck and Carter, in their introduction to *Psychology and Christianity: Integrative Readings*, stress that "relating Christianity to the thought forms and intellectual understandings of a society and culture is not new at all," but that "the integration of Christianity and psychology is very new. In fact, it is almost totally post-World War II, with most of the substantive work done in the last fifteen years" (p 15). Further, they observe that "one reason for the newness of integration with psychology is obviously that psychology itself is still quite young as a science, its birth customarily dated from the founding of a laboratory by Wundt in 1879" (p 15).

[25] In 1984, D. G. Benner wrote, "The last two decades have seen an enormous thawing in the climate of mistrust between Christianity and psychology" ["Psychology and Christianity" in *EDT* (Elwell, ed.), p 893].

[26] Compare Ellens' characterization of those who reject integration as invalid. In his critique of the term "integration" he states that the term unfortunately implies "at its base the essentially American-Fundamentalist notion that truth comes only through the Christian Scripture, by the special revealing action of the Holy Spirit of God." He goes on to aver that "[t]hat notion is a residuum of 'Old-Time Fundamentalism' in the schizophrenic way it sets the natural and supernatural worlds at odds, the apocalyptic way it demarcates the domain of God and of the demonic, and the pagan suggestion that lies at the bottom of this dichotomy, i.e., that God does not live here but must invade alien territory to enter the domain of 'this world' and its scientific truth" (Ellens, *CAPS* [1980:6:2], p 2). Ellens is able to interact with

But few would suggest that that cordial and accepting spirit is born of the persuasion that the work of integration has been accomplished to everyone's – indeed, to anyone's – satisfaction.[27] In fact, the recurring theme in the literature of the Christian Psychological community is that integration is a circle yet to be squared. The philosophical *commitment* to integration is unabated, and every integrationist model proceeds by definition upon the assumption that in some sense and to some degree that task has been at least provisionally accomplished. And yet it must be acknowledged that the task of integrating orthodox Christian theology with secular psychology, a task embarked upon with such heady optimism some twenty years ago, has proven itself disturbingly formidable. It is a Gordian knot yet untied.

The purpose of this article is to challenge certain working principles that impact many evangelically oriented attempts to integrate psychology and theology. However, it is necessary first of all to identify and define distinguishable *phases* of the effort at integration. That is, in the effort to erect a workable integration

---

confessionally anti-Christian secular psychologists without his indignation index ascending to heights anywhere near as dramatic as those evidently excited by his interaction with "Old-Time Fundamentalism."

[27] To be sure, there are individuals who have struggled with the issue of integrating Christianity and psychology and are personally satisfied that they have produced an epistemological construct which suffices, at least for their own purposes. But each of these constructs is widely criticized and corrected by others within the community, and most of those constructs are acknowledged to be partial and even tentative. Further, the work of integrating any system of thought as many-faceted and free-form as is Christian psychology with its counterpart in the secular world (which counterpart will be only more free-form given that it is not bounded by the delimiting factors native to Biblical Christianity) is by definition a perpetually unfinished business. So this statement is not intended to be negatively critical. It simply needs to be affirmed that within the Christian Psychological community the cart (models of counseling) has sometimes been allowed to run rather ahead of the horse (the epistemological construct which validates and controls the integrating impulse).

model which honors our commitment to Scripture as well as our commitment to help people in the most effective way possible, it is essential to begin by asking some questions which are *constituent* to that broader issue. The box below is suggested as a working construct within which the struggle to properly relate theology and psychology[28] can be conducted.

A Suggested Construct for Building an Integrationist Model
The Broad Issue: How can the individual who is committed to the Bible as the Word of God, and who is determined to help people as effectively as possible (and who suspects that there is some help to be found in the discipline of secular psychology) fashion a working schema of integration that will enable him to honor both his allegiance to Scripture and his commitment to helping others?
The Necessary and Interdependent Constituent Issues [to be read from the bottom up]

Phase II: The Procedural Question	Issue #3: *How* are theology and psychology best integrated? Note: This is a *methodological* issue. This question should only be addressed after the first two questions have both been answered affirmatively. This is where almost all of the integrationist work is being done today; the distinguishable theories are legion and the literature so broad as to be intimidating.
	"Water – Line"

---

[28] Throughout this article the term "psychology" will be employed with a deliberately narrow connotation, namely the "talk therapy" (or "psychotherapy") which is intrinsic to models of counseling embraced within the Christian psychological community. This is not to suggest that the term "psychology" does not have a broader significance, or that the criticisms leveled herein would apply with equal force or legitimacy to all aspects of that broader discipline. But in the integrationist literature the term is used consistently with the narrower significance of "talk therapy" as employed in personal counseling, and thus for ease of understanding the same nomenclature will be employed here.

Phase 1:
The Possibility Question
	Issue #2:
	    Ought theology and psychology to be integrated?
	    Note: This is an *ethical* issue. Not all things which *can* be done *should* be done. Is there any way in which the intrinsic virtue(s) and/or merit(s) of one discipline would be compromised or jeopardized by admixture with the other? Again, is there any intrinsic need or deficiency in theology which psychology can ameliorate? This question is moot unless the first question be answered in the affirmative.

	Issue #1:
	    Can theology and psychology be integrated?
	    Note: This is an *ontological* issue. That is, is there that in the essence of theology which makes it constitutionally incompatible with psychology, or vice versa?

Notice that this construct posits two distinguishable phases in the integrating effort. PHASE I deals with the Possibility question; that is, is there any possibility that an adequate integrating model can be developed; if so, is there ethical justification for doing so? PHASE II addresses the Procedural question: given that it can be done, how is it best done?

Further, notice that this construct is designed to emphasize that these constituent issues must be answered in a logical order. In fact, the arrangement in the box is intended to dramatize the reality that the question which most immediately suggests itself in the discussion of integration is the third one, the one that is "above the surface." And yet it is invalid to address the third question without first of all settling the issues reflected in the two questions below the line.

    The evangelical community has produced an intimidating body of literature intended to defend the proposition that the integration of psychology and theology is at once virtuous and possible, and to define how that integration might best be accomplished.[29] A survey of that literature suggests that three basic approaches prevail in the effort to integrate psychology and

---

[29] One of the most significant and seminal individual attempts to produce an integrative construct is that of G. R. Collins, *The Rebuilding of Psychology: An Integration of Psychology and Theology* (Wheaton, IL: Tyndale House, 1977). Collins focuses upon the world view and presuppositions which prevail in secular psychology; he attempts to displace or amend those with elements of a thoroughly Christian world view, thus redeeming the discipline from its own destructive foundation. For an early survey from *within* the Christian Psychological community of the efforts to define a workable model of integration, see J. D. Carter, "Secular and Sacred models of Psychology and Religion" in *Journal of Psychology and Theology*, 1977:5 (197-208); Carter reduces the models of integration to four, differentiated primarily to the degree that they presume an intrinsic and implacable antagonism between the world-views and/or the goals of secular psychology *vis a vis* orthodox Christian theology. The *Journal of Psychology and Theology* is sub-titled "An Evangelical Forum for the Integration of Psychology and Theology," and no issue is more often re-visited in its pages than that of integration. An article entitled "The Popularity of Integration Models, 1980-1985" [1988:16(1), 3-14] calculated that 43% of the articles published during that period (76 of 177 articles) addressed the issue. The entire Spring, 1980:8(1) issue is given over to an assessment of the progress of the integrating efforts from the inception of the journal in 1973 to the date of that issue. Further, the collection of essays edited by J. Roland Fleck and John D. Carter, *Psychology and Christianity: Integrative Readings* (Nashville: Abingdon, 1981) is very helpful, although one is perhaps most struck by the variety of models suggested and the manifest dissonance between many of them. *Wholehearted Integration: Harmonizing Psychology and Christianity Through Word and Deed*, by Kirk E. Farnsworth (Grand Rapids, MI: Baker Book House, 1985) has functioned as a watershed of sorts in the effort to define a workable schema for integration as well as to categorize the attempts. See also Larry Crabb, *Understanding People* (Grand Rapids, MI: Zondervan Publishing House, 1987), pp. 25-73 for an attempt to produce an integrative model which honors a high view of Scripture. A more recent extensive attempt at an integrationist construct from a committed evangelical perspective is *Modern Psycho-Therapies: A Comprehensive Christian Appraisal* by Stanton L. Jones and Richard E. Butman (Downers Grove, IL: InterVarsity Press, 1991). The most important critique of the integrationist effort by one not within the fold is that of David Powlinson, "Integration or Inundation?" in *Power Religion* (Chicago: Moody Press, 1992), Michael Scott Horton, ed., pp 191-218. Also important is Powlinson's "Which Presuppositions? Secular Psychology and the Categories of Biblical Thought" in *JPT* 1984: 12(4), pp 270-78. A consideration of the sundry efforts at integration

theology; the balance of this article will be a critique of those three. In the interest of integrity and fraternity, it is appropriate to acknowledge both the limitations of my expertise and the tentative character of this critique. I harbor no illusion that the questions and difficulties surrounding the integrationist effort will be solved in these pages. I am persuaded, however, that these three demand to be re-examined, along with the conclusion which is drawn from them.

Indeed, this article is born of a two-fold perception: first, the perception that every one of the three approaches which are so fundamental to the integrationist apologetic is seriously flawed in its validity and/or in its relevance to the issues at hand; and second, the realization that in spite of those perceived weaknesses many in the evangelical world have embraced one of these as a sufficient rationale for the notion that *the Scriptures alone are insufficient to help people who are hurting*! Surely, such a notion is not to be cavalierly embraced. The arguments which are appealed to in defense of that notion demand to be rigorously scrutinized. Thus this article.

The "Two-Book" Approach: Confused and Destructive

This fallacy relates to ISSUES #1 and #2 in the suggested construct; that is: "Can (#1) and Should (#2) theology and psychology be integrated?" Among those integrationists who confess a high view of Scripture, this specific claim functions more often than all others combined as the fundamental apologetic in defense of an affirmative reply to both of those ISSUES. Indeed,

---

lends abiding validity to the analysis of Berry in 1980 to the effect that "... as yet I do not discern much consensus as to what constitutes integration and how we are to achieve it" (C. Markham Berry, "Approaching the Integration of the Social Sciences and Biblical Theology," in *JPT*, Spring, 1980, p 33).

this affirmation is so often and confidently asserted that it has taken upon itself the identity of an axiom, a first truth so unassailable and self-evident as to demand only that it be expressed, never reasoned to or defended! In short, it is difficult to overstate the importance of this truth-claim in the foundation upon which the evangelical superstructure of integration has been erected.

The Argument Identified

The "two-book" fallacy may be reduced to the following propositions:

The Axiomatic Assertion:
All truth is God's truth.

The Theological Formulation:
God has made Himself known via two channels: special revelation and general revelation.

Special revelation is the propositional truth recorded in Scripture;

General revelation is non-propositional truth which is deposited by God in the created order of things and which must be investigated and discovered by man.

The Epistemological Conclusion:
Although the two channels of truth are distinguishable, both are in fact *revelatory*; thus truth accurately derived from the consideration of the natural order of things (general revelation) is just as "true" as that derived from Scripture.

49

The Integrationist Ramification:

> Any defensible *truth* which is derived by means of psychological research into the order of humanity is *truth* derived from general revelation, thus *truth* derived from God, and thus *truth* as dependable and authoritative as truth exegeted from Scripture.

Consider just a sampling of the expressions of this basic apologetic element by integrationist theorists. James D. Guy, Jr, in an article entitled "The Search for Truth in the Task of Integration" states,

> If integration is conceptualized as the search for truth concerning human nature, and God is identified as the source of this truth, the next logical issue involves the revelation of this truth. It has traditionally been held that God reveals this truth to us through both general and special revelation, with both nature and the Bible serving as expressions or representations of this truth. The disciplines of psychology and theology are attempts to discover and systematize truth by means of the study of the natural sciences and biblical revelation.[30]

Again, Fleck and Carter are quite explicit in this regard.

> Since God is the creator of the universe, all principles and laws have their origin in him. What is often called "nature" in science or philosophy is in reality God's creation. As his

---

[30] James D. Guy, Jr., "The Search for Truth in the Task of Integration," in *Journal of Psychology and Theology*, Spring, 1980, 8(1), p 28.

creation, nature and its laws reveal the Creator. Hence, theologians have referred to the picture of God in nature as general revelation because nature reveals God as a powerful and orderly creator. On the other hand, God is revealed in the Scripture and in Jesus Christ in a special way, i.e., special or particular details about God's person, nature, and his plan for human life and its relationship with him are revealed in Scripture. Hence, theologians refer to Scripture as special revelation.[31]

R. L. Timpe lays the same foundational rationale for the integration of theology and psychology.

> The task of integration involves an explicit relating of truth gleaned from general or natural revelation to that derived from special or biblical revelation, of interrelating knowledge gained from the world and knowledge gained from the Word....The integration movement offers a rapprochement by proposing the adoption of two premises: 1) God is the source of all truth no matter *where* it is found; 2) God is the source of all truth no matter *how* it is found. To the integrationist, natural revelation supports special revelation instead of being a rival methodology. That is, if God is consistent (i.e., immutable) as the Scriptures suggest (e.g., Mal. 3:6), then knowledge based in revelation should parallel and complement that derived from reason. Both will complement that founded in replication and observation. Underlying this approach is a faith statement

---

[31] J. Roland Fleck and John D. Carter, "Introduction," *Psychology and Christianity: Integrative Readings* (Nashville: Abingdon, 1981), p 18.

common to scientist and theologian alike: the laws that govern the operation of the world are discoverable.[32]

In the same vein, Ellens criticizes the "essentially American-Fundamentalist notion that truth comes only through the Christian Scriptures" because he feels it "devalues God's General Revelation in the world studied by the natural and social sciences" and thus "suggests that science, our reading of God's book in nature, is at war with the Christian Religion, our reading of God's other book, the Scriptures." Later in the same article Ellens avers,

> Theology and Psychology are both sciences in their own right, stand legitimately on their own foundations, read carefully are the two books of God's Revelation. They are not alien in any inherent sense....
> Wherever *truth* is disclosed it is always *God's truth*. Whether it is found in General Revelation or Special Revelation, it is *truth* which has equal warrant with all other *truth*. Some

---

[32] R. L. Timpe, "Christian Psychology" in *Baker Encyclopedia of Psychology* (Grand Rapids: Baker Book House, 1985), David G. Benner, ed., p 166 (emphasis original). The implication seems to be that those who reject the validity of the integrationist effort would also reject the two rather tautological premises, evidently because of a suspicion that findings of "truth" by the methodologies of natural science would not "support special revelation." The notion seems to be that to deny that "knowledge gained from the world" can possess intrinsic authority tantamount to that of "knowledge gained from the Word" is also to question whether "the laws that govern the operation of the world are discoverable." This is, very frankly, a canard which only muddies the water in the current debate. In an unpublished paper read at a regional meeting of the Evangelical Theological Association in 1991, John H. Coe takes the charge a step further, arguing that the non-integrationist fails in a stewardship God has given mankind to derive authoritative truth from nature, a stewardship reflected in the Old Testament sage's analysis of the natural order of things ("Educating the Church for Wisdom's Sake, or Why Biblical Counseling is Unbiblical," unpublished paper by John H. Coe, 1991).

truth may have greater weight than other *truth* in a specific situation, but there is no difference in its warrant as *truth*.[33]

Citations might be multiplied almost endlessly, but perhaps these will suffice to demonstrate the nature and importance of this specific rationale.[34]

---

[33] J. Harold Ellens, "Biblical Themes in Psychological Theory and Practice" in *CAPS* 1980:6(2), p. 2 (emphasis original). Ellens is actually criticizing the term "integration" here because he thinks the term suggests such a dichotomy. The canard only hinted at by Timpe (see former note) is by Ellens very explicitly and caustically laid against all non-integrationists. Of Jay E. Adams, Ellens remarks: "He apparently never even thought of the notion that all truth as God's truth, has equal warrant, whether truth from nature or scripture." Such a charge is simply ludicrous; Adams has written at rather copious lengths about this specific issue. (For a recent reference to the issue, see Adams' "Counseling and the Sovereignty of God" in *The Journal of Biblical Counseling* Winter, 1993:11[2], p. 6.) But notice how, in the mind of Ellens, this rationale has attained the status of a first truth; if a person does not submit to its validity and its ramifications, it can only be because he "never even thought of the notion"; the possibility that the notion is rejected because of a perceived flaw is not even entertained.

[34] It is interesting to see the same perceived fallacy involved in integrative efforts not immediately related to psychology/theology. For instance, in building a case for "Integrating Faith and Learning" in Christian Higher Education, Kenneth Gangel speaks of "natural revelation--science, mathematics, literature, music, etc." and goes on to say, "Many Christians tend to think of natural revelation only as the study of God's creation, but in reality all beauty is God's beauty just all truth is God's truth." He distinguishes that category of "natural revelation" from "Special Revelation: Bible/Theology" ("Integrating Faith and Learning: Principles and Process," in *BibSac*, April-June, 1978, p. 102). This is not meant as a criticism of the point being made in the article; it is simply to state that this fallacious definition of the theological concept of "general (here: natural) revelation" invades other disciplines as well.

The Argument Critiqued

The general revelation *vis a vis* special revelation argument is appealed to in the integrationist epistemological construct to support the proposition that integration *can* and *should* be done. However, that argument is crippled by the fact that the definition which is assigned the phrase "general revelation," and which is so foundational to the argument erected upon this term, is confused and erroneous on two counts: first it misdefines the term "revelation," and second it misdefines the term "general."

The Term "Revelation" is Misdefined

With reference to the term "revelation," this argument is flawed in that it neglects an element which is necessary to the Biblical concept, namely, that revelation is by definition *non-discoverable by human investigation or cogitation.*

This is the teaching of Scripture regarding God's communication of truth which we know as "revelation" (Isa 55:9; 1 Cor 2:11-14; 1 Tim 6:15,16; 2 Pet 1:19-21), and that teaching has been acknowledged and cherished by evangelical theologians. Chafer distinguishes sharply between reason and revelation, asserting that "revelation by its nature transcends the human capacity to discover and is a direct communication from God concerning truths which no person could discover by himself."[35]

---

[35] Lewis Sperry Chafer, *Systematic Theology: Abridged Edition*, John F. Walvoord, Editor (Wheaton, IL: Victor Books, 1988), I:63. Notice that revelation as being discussed here is a theological concept which "covers the semantic breadth of numerous biblical terms" (Clark H. Pinnock, *Biblical Revelation* [Chicago: Moody Press, 1971], p 29). B. B. Warfield discusses the range of terms in *The Inspiration and Authority of the Bible* [Philadelphia: Presbyterian and Reformed, 1948], pp 97-101. See also Bernard Ramm, *Special*

Erickson succinctly defines revelation as "[t]he making known of that which is unknown; the unveiling of that which is veiled."[36] Bancroft characterizes revelation as "that act of God by which He communicates to the mind of man truth not known before and incapable of being discovered by the mind of man unaided."[37] Thiessen emphasizes that same element of revelation in his definition: "By revelation we mean that act of God whereby He discloses Himself or communicates truth to the mind; whereby He makes manifest to His creatures that which could not be known in any other way."[38] Unger emphasizes this matter as well, characterizing the term "revelation" as "expressive of the fact that God has made known to men truths and realities which men could not discover for themselves."[39] And Pache labors to make the point that "revelation is of necessity an act of God."[40]

Revelation and the Word of God (Grand Rapids, MI: Eerdmans Publishing company, 1961), pp 161ff.

[36] Millard J. Erickson, *Concise Dictionary of Christian Theology* (Grand Rapids, MI: Baker Book House, 1986), p 143.

[37] Emery H. Bancroft, *Christian Theology* (Grand Rapids, MI: Zondervan Publishing House, 1955), p. 35.

[38] Henry C. Thiessen, *Introductory Lectures in Systematic Theology* (Grand Rapids, MI: Eerdmans Publishing Co, 1949), p. 31.

[39] M. F. Unger, "Revelation" in *Unger's Bible Dictionary* (Chicago: Moody Press, 1957), p 922.

[40] Rene Pache, *The Inspiration and Authority of Scripture*, Helen I. Needham, tran. (Chicago: Moody Press, 1969), p 13. I am aware that the above is a very superficial treatment of the nature of revelation, and that indeed that subject has been much debated as to its essence and extent. Specifically, the struggle as to the relationship between general revelation and natural theology, especially as it erupted among Christian thinkers after the Enlightenment, might be very germane to the issue at hand. Further, it is true that many theological definitions of the term "revelation" stop short of the element of non-

Over against this concept is the view native to the Two-Book theory that general *revelation* is truth which God has imbedded in the natural order and which man is responsible to extract from that order by investigation and cogitation. William F. English avers that

> ...the truths of general revelation are not delineated for us by God. Instead, they are "discovered" by fallible humans. At this point, it does not matter whether the "explorer" is a Christian or an atheist. Truths discovered in general revelation must be studied and examined for their trustworthiness, regardless of the religious beliefs of the giver.[41]

So there are two very different models of revelation before the house: one posits that God has made known certain truths to man, which truths man could never have discovered for himself; the other understands that God has somehow imbedded a myriad of

---

discoverability, affirming simply that the term means "the disclosure of what was previously unknown" (C. F. H. Henry, "Revelation, Special" in *Baker's Dictionary of Theology*, E. F. Harrison, ed. [Grand Rapids: Baker Book House, 1960], p 457). But the element of non-discoverability is usually latent in the discussion of the concept. At any rate, it can be argued that the Biblical description of the history and the idea of revelation demands that non-discoverability be acknowledged as a necessary element of the concept. Limitations of space forbid treatment of all the ancillary issues. The intent here is very narrow: simply to get the reader to confront what seems to be a basic contradiction in meaning between the orthodox understanding of the theological concept of revelation and the meaning assigned the term when it is employed as part of the rationale for the integrationist effort.

[41] William F. English, "An Integrationist's Critique of and Challenge to the Bobgan's View of Counseling and Psychotherapy," in *JPT*, 1990:18(3), p 229.

truths in the natural order and that man is capable of and responsible for ferreting out those truths.

Now it is at this point that the intent of my argument is most liable to misunderstanding and thus must be very carefully expressed. For the record, I will enthusiastically affirm each of the following propositions:

[1] that God *is* the Author and Sustainer of the created order;

[2] that there *are* facts and realities and truths which by means of human investigation and cogitation are to be discovered in the created order, both natural and human;

[3] that the possibility exists that such humanly discovered and verified facts and realities are no less true than truth communicated directly by God;[42]

[4] that many of the facts and verities thus discovered by man's investigation into the created order can be employed to help people in many ways.

The issue, then, is not whether it is possible that truth might be discovered by human investigation of the natural and moral universe; rather, the issue is whether truth thus discovered can legitimately be assigned to the category of general revelation.

My contention is that by reason of the proper definition of the theological category "general revelation" and by reason of the intrinsic and divine integrity and authority which must be granted to any truth-claim which is placed under that category, it is erroneous and misleading to assign to that category humanly deduced and/or discovered facts and theories. The issue is larger

---

[42] Indeed, the very notion of degrees of "truth," of some "truths" being more "true" than other "truths," is definitionally erroneous.

than appropriate taxonomy.[43] In fact, to assign such humanly determined truths to the category of general revelation introduces a two-fold fallacy into the argument when it is used as a rationale for the integrationist position.

First, there is the fallacy which might be termed *falsely perceived validity*. Revelation is from God; thus it is by definition true and authoritative. To assign man's discoveries to the category of general revelation is to imbue them with an aura of validity and consequent authority which they do not, indeed, they cannot merit. Thus, to assign a concept to the category of "general revelation" when that concept is in fact a theory concocted by man is in effect to lend God's name to man's ideas. That is fallacious, *no matter the intrinsic truth or falsehood of the truth-claim under consideration.*

The second fallacy involved in thus construing as general revelation those perceived truths which are discovered by man might be called *crippled accountability*. That is, once it is acknowledged that these theories are *revelatory* in nature, they have been rendered functionally beyond reproach. Much may be said about testing the ideas thus derived before acknowledging them as part of that august body of truth which God has communicated in the natural order of things, or about honoring the distinction in

---

[43] In fact, the misdefinition being discussed here does involve an error with reference to taxonomy (i.e., the assignment of entities and concepts to appropriate categories). That error is the mistaken assumption that the categories "truth" and "revelation" are co-terminus. In fact, all revelation is truth, but not all truth is revelation. In other words, *truth* is a larger category than is *revelation*; this is why we speak of "revealed truth" (as opposed to truth which is not ours by revelation but by investigation). This is not to disparage revealed truth; indeed, although revealed truth is not any more TRUE than discovered truth, it is more DEPENDABLE, simply because it is made known to us directly by God.

intrinsic authority between general and special revelation;[44] but to craft an argument for integration based upon the equal merits and authority of general revelation and special revelation is functionally to short-circuit such efforts and to deny such distinctions. Very simply, if it is revelation, then God said it; if God said it, then it is true; when God speaks truth, man's responsibility is *not to test that truth but to obey it.* It is self-contradictory to insist that general *revelation* can include *truths* which must be "studied and examined for their trustworthiness."[45]

In summary, then, the integrationist rationale which arises from the claim that perceived truths established by human research constitute a sub-set of the category general revelation, and thus possess the authority and dependability native to revelation, is flawed first of all in its misdefinition of the term "revelation." Inherent to the biblical concept of revelation is the idea of non-discoverability, but the most dominant element of general revelation as construed in this rationale is that the facts to be granted the status of revelation are by definition the result of human research and observation.

---

[44] For instance, English speaks of "the lesser truths of general revelation" (*Ibid*, p 231). But this distinction between the lesser authority of general revelation and the greater authority of special revelation is an invalid and perilous distinction. To posit degrees of authority and dependability between various channels of revelation is very dangerous. In fact all revelation is from God, and thus all revelation is absolutely true and, assuming proper hermeneutical treatment, normative. Again, this error is born of a misdefinition of the very idea of revelation.

[45] English, *JPT* 1990:18(3), p 229.

Second, the "two-book" theory is flawed in its misdefinition of the term "general." In the articulation of the "two-book" argument, it is clear from the use to which the term "general" is put, and sometimes from the accompanying explication and application of the concept, that the term is to be taken to signify "generic, non-specific as to category or verifiability, cutting across a broad spectrum of loosely related topics." (This in contrast to "special" revelation, which term is conceived to connote "narrow or specific as to category and focus, dealing with but one category.")

According to Fleck and Carter, for instance, general revelation is so called because it communicates the "picture of God in nature." The contrast to special revelation is represented thus: "God is revealed in the Scripture and in Jesus Christ in a special way, i.c., special or particular details about God's person, nature, and his plan for human life and its relationship with him are revealed in Scripture." Notice that it is because special or specific details are revealed in Scripture that "theologians refer to Scripture as special revelation."[46]

This is a critical misunderstanding of the connotation intended for the term "general" in this phrase. It makes the referent of the descriptive force of the term to be the *content of the revelation* thus described. In fact, as the term *"general* revelation" is historically and universally employed in evangelical theology, the term "general" is intended to characterize not the character of revelation under discussion but the audience to whom that

---

[46] Fleck and Carter, Ibid., p 18.

revelation is available. Ryrie describes the "Characteristics of General Revelation" as follows:

> General revelation is exactly that--general. It is general in its scope; that is, it reaches to all people (Matt 5:45; Acts 14:17). It is general in geography; that is, it encompasses the entire globe (Ps 19:2). It is general in its methodology; that is, it employs universal means like the heat of the sun (vv. 4-6) and human conscience (Rom 2:14-15). Simply because it is a revelation that thus affects all people wherever they are and whenever they have lived, it can bring light and truth to all, or if rejected, brings condemnation.[47]

So general revelation is characterized as "general" not because it deals with a broad and non-specific (that is, general) category of facts, but because it is accessible to all men of all time (that is, to men *generally*).

Again, *special* revelation is so-called not because it makes known "special or particular details about God's person, nature, and his plan for human life,"[48] but because it is made known not generally but to specific individuals. Thiessen distinguishes special

---

[47] Charles C. Ryrie, *Basic Theology* (Wheaton, IL: Victor Books, 1988), p 28. Compare Erickson's concise definition of **"Revelation, General.** Revelation which is available to all persons at all times..." (Erickson, *Ibid*, p 143). Thiessen identifies the distinguishing element of general revelation as the fact that "it is addressed to all intelligent creatures generally and is accessible to all" (Thiessen, *Ibid*, p 32). Demerast defines general revelation as the "divine disclosure to all persons at all times and places by which one comes to know that God is and what he is like" (B. A. Demarest, "Revelation, General" in *EDT*, p 944).

[48] Fleck and Carter, Ibid, p 18.

revelation as "those acts of God whereby He makes Himself and His truth known at special times and to specific peoples."[49] So the integrationist apologetic which takes the term *general* in general revelation as referring to the type of content which can be placed under that category, and therefore argues that all manner of sundry facts and realities derived by human investigation can thus be categorized, is rendered fallacious by its misdefinition of the term *general*.[50]

And that fallacy is ominous on two counts. First, it is perilous because it *expands the category* known as general revelation far beyond what Scripture allows. Demarest and Harpel define the extent of the truth which is divinely disclosed through the channel of general revelation as "(a) a metaphysical dualism--that a supreme Creator exists distinct from finite creatures; (b) an ethical dualism--that there is a difference between right and wrong; and (c) an epistemological dualism--that truth exists as distinct from error."[51] It is a category carefully restricted by the teachings of

---

[49] Thiessen, Ibid, p 35. Compare Erickson's definition: "God's manifestation of himself at particular times and places through particular events..." (*Ibid*, p 144). Demarest characterizes special revelation by the fact that "God sovereignly disclosed His redemptive purposes to certain people" (Bruce A. Demarest and Richard J. Harpel, "'Redemptive Analogies' and the Biblical Idea of Revelation," *Bibliotheca Sacra*, July-September, 1989, p 336).

[50] This is not to insist that the misdefinition at hand *proves* that the category "general revelation" could not be expansive enough to include all those perceived realities (though it is my persuasion that it cannot). The limits of the category "general revelation" must be established by appeal to the Scriptures (see below). However, it needs to be emphasized that the misunderstanding concerning the term "general" is at the heart of the axiomatic use to which the phrase is put, and it is that axiomatic force which is entirely broken by the observation that the term is being misdefined.

[51] Demarest and Harpel, Ibid, p 335. For a careful development of the dangers of expanding the category of general revelation, see Kenneth Kantzer,

Scripture, and orthodox theology has honored the Biblical bounds placed upon it. It is general in that it includes revelation available to all men, but it is not a *general* category sufficient to include all the discoveries and theories of human reasoning.

Again, the fallacy implicit in the definition of this term is destructive because it *eviscerates the character* of general revelation. That is, as described in Scripture, general revelation is truth which is manifestly set forth before all men (Rom 1:17-19; 2:14,15); it is truth so clear and irrefutable as to be known intuitively by all rational men[52] (Ps 19:1-6; Rom 1:19); it is truth so authoritative and manifest that when men, by reason of willful rebellion, reject that truth, they do so at the cost of their own eternal damnation (Rom 1:20; 2:1,15). For this seamless, flawless and majestic tapestry of God-given truth is substituted a patchwork of "lesser"[53] truths, of truth which "is obtainable at least in part,"[54] truths which "are not delineated for us by God" but are "discovered by fallible humans" and thus must be "studied and examined for their trustworthiness,"[55] truth the consideration of which "hopefully results in a higher level of insight and understanding."[56] Surely

---

"The Communication of Revelation," in *The Bible: The Living Word of Revelation*, Merrill C. Tenney, ed (Grand Rapids, MI: Zondervan Publishing House, 1968), pp. 62-69.

[52] A concept admirably and succinctly reduced to the title of a very helpful book by J, Budziszewski, *What We Can't Not Know* (Spence Publishing Company, Dallas TX, 2003).

[53] English, *JPT* 1990:18(3), p 231.

[54] Stephen M. Clinton, "The Foundational Integration Model" in *JPT* 1990:18(2), p 117.

[55] English, *JPT* 1990:18(3), p 229.

[56] Guy, *JPT* 1980:8(1), p 27.

such a concept of general revelation represents a ravaging of the biblical concept.

Not every integrationist apologetic employs the argument from the nature of general revelation, but most do. Further, the more thoroughly and visibly evangelical the apologist, the more likely he is to employ that argument. But it has been the contention here that the two-book approach is twice flawed. First, it is <u>confused</u> in its definition of the term "revelation." By defining general revelation as that body of truth which is gained by human investigation and discovery, the argument is guilty of neglecting the element of non-discoverability which is intrinsic to the biblical notion of revelation and supplanting that notion with its exact antithesis. Further, the approach is <u>dangerous</u> in that it attributes to the truth-claims of men an authority which they do not and cannot possess, and renders it virtually impossible to bring those truth-claims under the authority of the one standard by which God demands that they be measured.

Second, the argument from the perceived authoritative character of general revelation is <u>confused</u> in its definition of the term "general." By mistakenly taking that term to refer to the *content* of the category (rather than to the *audience* to which the revelation thus denominated is available), the apologists who employ this argument commit two fallacies which are <u>destructive</u> of orthodox theology: first, they expand the category to include all manner of truth-claims which have no right to be thus honored; and second, they eviscerate the character of revelation by including in the category truth-claims which are admittedly lesser than the truths of Scripture, which demand that finite and fallen men measure them to determine their validity, and which at best can *possibly* issue in a higher level of insight into the demands of living.

In summary, I am persuaded that, in the interest of validating the integrationist impulse and effort, many in the

Christian psychological community have, wittingly or unwittingly, exchanged the biblical doctrine of general revelation for one of their own making. The evangelical world is entirely the loser in the bargain.

The "No-Book" Approach: Corrupt and Dishonest

This perceived fallacy is not nearly so prevalent as the one discussed above, and it tends to be embraced by those with less of a commitment to the inerrant character of Scripture. However, as one moves forward in time this mentality is encountered with increasing frequency across the integrationist spectrum.

The Approach Identified

The "No-Book" approach may be reduced to the following propositions:

The Axiomatic Affirmation:
All truth-sources are liable to produce error to the degree that fallible and pre-conditioned men are involved in accessing those sources.

The Theological Formulation:
Regardless of the intrinsic truthfulness and consequent authority of Scripture, any human application of Scripture presupposes the process of interpretation.

By reason of spiritual fallenness and cultural/gender pre-conditioning, man necessarily comes to the interpretative task laboring under significant and crippling liabilities.

The Epistemological Conclusion:

All human knowledge is flawed by definition. There is no reason to be any *more* suspicious of science than of theology (i.e., of the theories and facts derived by human investigation and deduction than of supposed truths derived from Scripture) simply because Scripture is no *less* liable to the limitations of human participation than is any other truth-source.

Regardless of the authority and/or verity of the truth-source, man's *knowing* of truth can only approach greater and greater levels of probability; certainty is presuppositionally unthinkable.

The Integrationist Ramifications:

Negatively, any suggestion that finality or certainty might be imputed to any element of any model is mistaken.

Positively, the integrationist must be constantly testing and refining all of his findings and convictions, from the presuppositional to the methodological, in the hope that he can effect for himself an ascending spiral of confidence and effectiveness.

This is rather a stark and perhaps disquieting expression of the fallacy under consideration. But in fact this is the essence of the position being taken by many in the integrationist community.

For instance, in addressing the question, "Can We Know the Truth?", Guy acknowledges that the Scriptures "reveal ultimate truth about mankind and our existence," but goes on to warn that "[a]ttempts to know the truth as it is revealed through the Bible are prone to the same errors and inaccuracies found in the observation and interpretation of truth as it is revealed through nature."[57] He argues from the "existence of numerous, conflicting, and constantly changing theories about truth" that "we are unable to fully know the truth since our knowledge is partial, at best."[58] This line of reasoning leads Guy to the following implication:

> Because we are unable to know the truth and our attempts to do so are prone to error, the conclusions of theology are prone to the same errors as those made when formulating the conclusions of science. Neither set of theories about truth needs to have ultimate authority over the other. Assumptions about the truth as it is revealed in the Bible

---

[57] James D. Guy, Jr, "The Search for Truth in the Task of Integration," *JPT* Spring, 1980:8(1), p. 29. Guy has affirmed in the context that "God reveals...truth to us through both general and special revelation, with both nature and the Bible serving as expressions of this truth" (p 28). He regards the two as fully equal in authority and dependability. It is interesting that he employs the "two-book" argument at the axiomatic level, but his view of both "books" (nature and the Bible) manifests an even more thoroughly impoverished understanding of the concept of revelation.

[58] Guy, p 30. This entire article is a response to Collins' attempt to construct a model of integration (G.D. Collins, *The Rebuilding of Psychology: An Integration of Psychology and Theology* [Wheaton: Tyndale House, 1977]). Guy's argument is that Collins' has erred in supposing that any one model of integration could be intrinsically superior to all others.

need not be regarded as authoritative over the assumptions of science. If God is, indeed, the source of all revealed truth, any apparent contradiction is the result of error in observation or interpretation of that truth in the disciplines of science or theology, or both. Because error is probable in either field, diversity can be viewed as a stimulus for growth and development--a process which hopefully will result in higher levels of accuracy and understanding in the search for truth.[59]

Finally, in an attempt to put a happier spin on this rather discouraging epistemology, Guy concludes,

> There will be no single model of integration, nor will there be one set of therapeutic assumptions, techniques, or goals which are totally accurate and true. Christian psychologists are free to adopt any one of a variety of models and orientations as they seek to work out a personal integration within the scope of their own private ministries.[60]

It is because of this sort of conclusion that this mentality is here denominated the No-Book fallacy. Very simply, this construct leaves the counseling community with no book, no authority, no absolutely dependable source of truth, no normative standard against which to measure the countless theories and models proffered today in the worlds of psychology and counseling.

Thorson posits this same epistemological limitation: "...the important fact that a divine revelation is the real *source* of our

---

[59] Guy, p 31.

[60] Guy, p 31.

knowledge does not eliminate the purely epistemological problems of communication, interpretation, and comprehension, nor does it impart a special status of rational certainty to our knowledge itself."[61] Farnsworth articulates a similar mentality. Appealing to an article in which it is argued that "male dominance has tarnished even our best translations [of the Bible],"[62] from which he derives evidence of the inescapable pre-conditioning which inexorably discolors any understanding of even an authoritative text, Farnsworth concludes that "[i]n spite of the accessibility of the words of Scripture, reading them is not a matter of perfect perception. It is easy to forget that reading the Bible is a psychological-perceptual experience."[63] He goes on to add this methodological caveat.

> Since God reveals his truths in a variety of ways, various disciplines other than theology are needed to interpret the wide range of revelational data. Further, since all academic disciplines are subject to human error, no one discipline should be made subservient to any other. What I am *not*

---

[61] W. R. Thorson, "The Biblical Insights of Michael Polanyi, *Journal of the American Scientific Affiliation*, 1981, 33, p 132, (emphasis original).

[62] B. Mickelsen and A. Mickelsen, "Does Male Dominance Tarnish Our Translations?", *Christianity Today*, October 5, 1979, pp 23-29.

[63] Kirk E. Farnsworth, "The Conduct of Integration," in *JPT* Winter, 1982:10(4), p 311. Shepperson, in replying to the article by Farnsworth, makes mention of the "assumption that one's experiential base, conscious and unconscious, influences one's perception of theological and psychological truth" as part of his argument that theology should not exercise "imperialism" over psychology (Vance L. Shepperson, "Systemic Integration: A Reactive Alternative to 'The Conduct of Integration'," *JPT* 1982:10(4), p 326). Shepperson expresses delight that Farnsworth's article "indicates a willingness to evenly weight multiple inputs from various disciplines."

saying is that the Bible does not have functional authority over all other forms of revelation. What I am saying is that theology, as a human discipline, does not necessarily have functional authority over any other human discipline.[64]

The No-Book approach becomes most manifest and alarming when it is employed in the development of an integrationist apologetic for the veracity and authority of "truth" derived from psychological research. First, it often becomes the means of effecting the *de facto* denial of the role which the Scriptures have normally been expected to play in an evangelically oriented system of thought. For instance, in an attempt to frame a Christian epistemology, the following warning is issued.

> Revelation as a source of knowledge presupposes a transcendent supernatural reality. Christian education argues that truth gained through this source is absolute. However, one must realize that distortion of this truth is possible in the process of human interpretation. Therefore, the Christian must be careful not to become preoccupied with revelation and fail to use the other sources of knowledge available in seeking truth.[65]

---

[64] Farnsworth, p 311 (emphasis original). Notice again the axiomatic expression of the "two-book" fallacy in the use of the phrase "other forms of revelation" in reference to other human disciplines. This distinction between the Bible and theology, between the authoritative truth-source and the fallible accessor of that source, is vacuous; it will be discussed below.

[65] Jimmy F. Sellars, "In Defense of a Christian Epistemology," *Christian Education Journal*, Spring 1992:12(3), p 163. The "other sources of knowledge" which Sellars catalogues in the article are "reason, intuition, the senses, and the secondary source of testimony or authority" (p 163).

Earlier in the article the author had affirmed the importance and uniqueness of Scripture, but here he cripples the role which those Scriptures can play by reminding his reader that "distortion of this truth is possible in the process of human interpretation."[66]

Second, the corrupting influence of the No-Book approach is seen in the fact this argument--which insists that though the Scriptures might indeed be absolutely true and authoritative, any human understanding of those Scriptures will necessarily be tarnished by limitations intrinsic to man--might be expected to issue in a certain carelessness about the interpretation of Scripture. That is, if the interpreter knows that no matter how much effort he expends in the attempt, his work will always be so flawed *as to disqualify his conclusions as a standard of truth,* he is left with no compelling incentive to heroic diligence in the stewardship of interpretation. Very simply, if the results of careful exegesis can

---

[66] Compare James D. Foster and Mark Ledbetter, "Christian Anti-Psychology and the Scientific Method", *JPT* 1987:15(1), p 17, where after a discussion concerning "what is the most valuable way of knowing" they conclude, "While we can accept authority, intuition, and personal experience as valuable approaches to learning, we object when knowledge from these sources is presumed in some way to be superior to knowledge gained through observation, measurement, and experimentation." Earlier the authors had acknowledged that "the Bible is...an authority to Christians because of its revelatory nature" (p 11). This evisceration of the Scriptures' authoritative role comes full in Morton Kelsey's "Reply to Analytical Psychology and Human Evil [*JPT* 1986:14(4), 282-84], in which the author argues that the "thinking and experience" of C. G. Jung "provide the best framework upon which to base the integration of psychology and theology" (p 282). Kelsey is responding to G. A. Elmer Griffin's "Analytical Psychology and the Dynamics of Human Evil: A Problematic Case in the Integration of Psychology and Theology" [*JPT* 1986:14(4), 269-77], in which Griffin critiques a series of lectures at Fuller Theological Seminary in which Kelsey argued that Jung could best serve as the "framework" for integrating psychology and theology. The point is, of course, that the Scriptures have here been displaced by Jung as a framework for accomplishing integration.

possess no greater intrinsic authority than the results of sloppy exegesis, there is no reason to do careful exegesis.

Whether it is fair to *anticipate* this fall-out from the No-Book mentality, the reader will decide for himself. But it is my observation that an alarmingly cavalier attitude toward exegesis does in fact surface with disturbing regularity in the writings of the "no-book" theorists.

For instance, in arguing for "nonrational" or "humanistic psychological and theological methodologies" which would "allow us to ask questions unrestricted by our natural scientific technology and rationalistic theological categories," Farnsworth makes some rather creative use of Scripture.

> The nonrational is the sensitivity of feeling that balances the sensibleness of rationality and that gives warmth and richness to the direction and maturity of reason. It is the direct preconceptual encounter with God that enables one to pray in silent expectancy...and without ceasing (1 Thessalonians 5:17)....This is what Jeremiah meant, saying, "But let the one who glories boast in this, that he understands and knows Me" (Jeremiah 9:24).[67]

In a reply to Farnsworth in the same edition of *JPT*, Virkler chastens him for using the Scriptures "carelessly," and briefly examines the two passages appealed to by Farnsworth, concluding that "by no stretch of our exegetical imaginations" can those

---

[67] Farnsworth, "Conduct of Integration," *JPT* Winter, 1982:10(4), p 312.

passages be used as Farnsworth had used them.[68] Farnsworth responds as follows:

> I can see how [Virkler], being an expert in the area of hermeneutics, could form a negative opinion about my hermeneutics, when he sees that we disagree on the meaning of certain portions of Scripture. Although I agree that this is in fact a minor criticism that does not detract from the validity of my integration model, I disagree that because we do not agree on the rendering of some verses of Scripture I am "careless" and he is not. There is no basis whatever in my article for such a judgment.[69]

He makes no attempt to defend his understanding of the passages through hermeneutical considerations; he simply asserts that he disagrees with his critic's understanding of those same passages. In fact, there is no defense of Farnsworth's use of those passages except this: the way he construes those biblical texts supports the point he is trying to make in the article. The prosecution rests.

---

[68] Henry A. Virkler, "Response to `The Conduct of Integration" *JPT*, 1982:10(4), p 332.

[69] Farnsworth, "Responses to `The Conduct of Integration": An Appreciative Reaction", *JPT*, 1982:10(4), p 334. The "basis" in Farnsworth's article for Virkler's "judgment" of poor hermeneutics is simply the fact that Farnsworth makes the passages to which he appeals say something very different than, if not antithetical to, the plain meaning of those passages in their contexts. This is precisely the criticism lodged by Virkler, but it has no force whatever in the mind of Farnsworth. The suggestion is that, given the approach employed by Farnsworth, exacting hermeneutics have not only ceased to be a possibility, they have ceased to be a consideration.

The Approach Critiqued

The No-Book approach is ultimately corruptive of the very notion of epistemological authority, and thus of the possibility of *functional* absolutes in the moral realm. That is, the Scriptures (it is acknowledged) may (probably, "do") possess *intrinsic* truth which will, in some entirely transcendental other-world, exercise authority in the cosmic struggle of competing truth-claims. But because man's every attempt to comprehend the meaning of those Scriptures is prejudged as crippled and crippling, and because in the contest of ideas appeal can be made only to man's understanding of the Scriptures (as opposed to the raw material of their intrinsic meaning), the Scriptures cannot *functionally* referee between competing truth-claims.

In a discussion of the idea that there is a "running throughout Scripture" some "radical obscurity, or outright incoherence, or at least a Delphic[70] sort of ambiguity," Packer comes to a similar conclusion concerning the necessary implications of such a notion.

> Ought we then to conclude that when the Reformers affirmed the intrinsic clarity of Scripture in presenting its central message, they were wrong and that the many millions who down the centuries have lived and died by the light of what they took to be divinely taught certainties were self-deceived? Must we say that no such certainties are

---

[70] The reference is to the Grecian Oracle at Delphi, a supposed soothsayer who deliberately couched her prognostications in ambiguous pictures and phrases so as to eliminate the possibility that any votary might challenge her accuracy.

available to us, nor ever were to anyone? That is what this idea, if accepted, would imply.[71]

The Scriptures have often been thus characterized as intrinsically ambiguous and therefore non-authoritative, but the charge has come from those who would deny the high view of the inerrancy and authority of Scripture which has been a hall-mark of evangelical theology.[72] To find the same pejorative assessment of Scripture coming from the pens of those who claim evangelical credentials "cannot but disturb."[73]

In fact, however, the notion that "purely epistemological problems of communication, interpretation, and comprehension"[74] render the authority of Scripture an irrelevancy is fatally flawed on at least three counts. First, it is logically fallacious and dishonest.

---

[71] J. I. Packer, "Infallible Scripture and the Role of Hermeneutics," in *Scripture and Truth*, Gerard Terpstra, ed. (Grand Rapids, MI: Zondervan Publishing House, 1983), p 329. In this section of his article (which section is entitled "Has Scripture One Clear Message?"), Packer is directly addressing the mentality at the base of the No-Book mentality, namely the contention that "the method of appeal and submission to Scripture, no matter how carefully pursued, is intrinsically unable to produce certainty," and this because, as is claimed, "modern insight into the hermeneutical process shows that different things are conveyed to different people by the same texts, depending on where those people are coming from and what experience and questions they bring with them..." (p 328). After very careful consideration of that mentality, Packer concludes that "such arguments as are currently offered to prove the intrinsic incoherence, ambiguity, or unintelligibility of Scripture...are very far from successful" (p 332).

[72] In introducing his discussion of what is referred to in this article as the No-Book mentality, Packer observes that "liberal theology has long maintained" such an attitude toward the Scriptures (Packer, Ibid., p 328).

[73] Packer, Ibid., p 329.

[74] Thorson, Ibid., p 132.

Human language is being employed by the detractor to insist that knowable thoughts cannot be communicated via human language. This is the sky-writer who mounts to the heavens in his bi-plane to scrawl across the horizon the message, "Human flight is impossible!" The No-Book theorist uses thousands of words to insist that words can mean nothing for certain. The thesis is disproven by its very articulation. As Pinnock observes,

> The argument is fallacious and self-defeating....On purely logical grounds, if a person's interpretation is invalid simply because it is *his* interpretation, then the objector's opinion is wrong because it is *his* opinion.[75]

Second, the No-Book mentality is a denial of the doctrine classically known as the *perspicuity* of Scripture, defined as "clarity of thought, lucidity," and identified as "one of the traditional attributes of Scripture."[76] Hodge reduces the doctrine of perspicuity to the simple affirmation that "The Bible is a plain book...intelligible by the people." [77] The Westminster Confession (1.7) articulates this doctrine as follows:

---

[75] Clark Pinnock, *Biblical Revelation* (Chicago: Moody Press, 1971), p 99. The specific argument to which Pinnock has reference here is that which claims "that the interpretation of any text is a matter of personal opinion, and that certain knowledge of what the Bible says is impossible" (p 99). This is in a section in which Pinnock is contending for the "Clarity" of Scripture, and which begins with the affirmation that "[i]t is necessary for Scripture, if it is to be our authority, to be clear so that we can read and understand it" (p 97).

[76] Richard A. Muller, *Dictionary of Latin and Greek Theological Terms: Drawn Principally from Protestant Scholastic Theology* (Grand Rapids, MI: Baker Book House, 1985), p 228. By "traditional attributes" Muller means that this is a characteristic traditionally attributed to Scripture in Protestant theology.

[77] Charles Hodge, *Systematic Theology: Abridged Edition*, Edward N. Gross,

All things in Scripture are not alike plain in themselves, nor alike clear unto all, yet those things which are necessary to be known, believed and observed for salvation, are so clearly propounded and opened in some place of Scripture or other, that not only the learned, but the unlearned, in a due use of ordinary means, may attain unto a sufficient understanding of them.

Although in the history of Christian doctrine the canon of perspicuity, or clarity, was worked out in the context of a very different struggle,[78] the principles involved apply immediately and necessarily to the No-Book mentality. Indeed, this doctrine of clarity (or perspicuity) stands in judgment upon any claim that the Bible is incomprehensible by men *for any reason relating to the character or accessibility of the Bible.* As Pinnock observes, "An obscure book could not perform the functions Scripture would perform. A denial of perspicuity is a denial of the *sola scriptura* principle itself."[79]

---

ed. (Grand Rapids, MI: Baker Book, 1988), p 92.

[78] The doctrine of perspicuity was articulated by the Reformers in denial of the Roman Catholic claim that "the Bible is obscure, and is badly in need of interpretation even in matters of faith and practice." According to Berkhof, the contention of the Reformers "was simply that the knowledge necessary unto salvation, though not equally clear on every page of Scripture, is yet conveyed to man throughout the Bible in such a simple and comprehensible form that one who is earnestly seeking salvation can, under the guidance of the Holy Spirit, by reading and studying the Bible, easily obtain for himself the necessary knowledge, and does not need the aid and guidance of the Church and of a separate priesthood" (L. Berkhof, *Introductory Volume to Systematic Theology* [Grand Rapids, MI: Eerdmans Publishing Company, 1932], p 167). Compare the "modified" analysis of this Reformational struggle in G. C. Berkouwer, *Holy Scripture* (Grand Rapids, MI: Eerdmans Publishing Company, 1975), pp 271-73.

[79] Pinnock, Ibid., p 99.

The evangelical community ought to regard with radical suspicion the tendency of the No-Book theorist to cavalierly reject a concept as central to the Protestant tradition as the doctrine of the perspicuity of Scripture.

Third, the No-Book mentality is denied by Scripture itself on several counts.

1) The Bible affirms that men will be held eternally accountable for disobeying the teachings contained therein (Ps 50:16,17; Prov 13:13; Isa 5:24; Luke 24:25; 2 Tim 4:3,4) and that obedience to those words will result in temporal and eternal blessedness (Jms 1:18; 2 Tim 3:15,16). It is absurd to suppose that God would promise to punish those who disobey, or to bless those who obey, words which by nature can at best attain only to "a Delphic sort of ambiguity."[80] Indeed, Jesus commanded His contemporaries to "search the Scriptures" (Jn 5:39), assuming that those hearers "were able to understand what the Old Testament said of the Messiah, although its teachings had been misunderstood by the scribes and elders and by the whole Sanhedrin."[81]

2) The messages and books of the Bible are addressed in context to people with the expectation that those people will obey and understand. Indeed, in the narratives of the Bible, the generation who first received the messages are held accountable for their willingness to obey. Hodge insists that

---

[80] Packer, Ibid., p 329.

[81] Hodge, Ibid., p 94.

> It is the people who are addressed....They are
> everywhere assumed to be competent to understand
> what is written and are everywhere required to
> believe and obey what thus comes from the inspired
> messengers of Christ.[82]

3)   The message of Scripture was regarded as so plain that the
recipients were commanded to "teach them diligently unto
thy children" (Deut 6:7) and unto "thy son's sons" (Deut
4:9).

4)   The Scriptures repeatedly make the claim to be plain and
accessible by men.

> Scripture is a "light shining in a dark place (2 Pe
> 1:19). The "Father of lights" has give His Word to
> be a lamp to our feet and a light to our path (Ps
> 119:105). It is not inaccessible and hidden from us
> (Deu 30:11-14). We are commanded to read and
> search it (Jn 5:39; Ac 17:11). It makes wise the
> simple, revives the soul, rejoices the heart,
> enlightens the eyes (Ps 19:7, 8). Scripture is clear
> because it is *God's*. If it were not clear, it would fail
> in its intention.[83]

Again, far from allowing the notion of their own intrinsic
ambiguity, Scriptures suggest that the denial of the clarity

---

[82] Hodge, Ibid., p 93.

[83] Pinnock, Ibid., p 98.

and thus of the authority of the Bible is born of the impulse to reject God's authority, which in turn is born of wicked rebellion (Prov 1:29,30; Isa 30:9; Jn 3:20).

Denial of clarity reflects a refusal to be bound by Scripture and a determination to follow one's own inclinations. Whenever a church or a theologian takes it upon himself to define truth without reference to the objective authority of God's Word, he becomes demonically solipsistic.[84]

In sum, the No-Book approach insists that, by reason of the limitations native to the human interpreter, no *more* can be said of the dependability and authority of Scripture than can be said of any other alleged truth source. This approach is a deconstructionist wolf in the clothing of an evangelical sheep.[85] It is corrupt in its essence and in its implications; it is dishonest in that it denies to the words of Scripture the measure of plainness and meaning which the theorist assumes for his own words; it is antithetical to a doctrine which is cardinal to the theological tradition which lays behind the evangelical movement; it is contradicted and condemned by the *plain* teachings of Scripture.

---

[84] Pinnock, Ibid., p 99. By "solipsistic" Pinnock means the spirit which regards nothing but self as important.

[85] See the discussion of "Deconstructionism" in Tremper Longman, *Literary Approaches to Biblical Interpretation* (Grand Rapids: Zondervan Publishing House, 1987), pp 41-45.

The "Rule-Book" Approach: Commendable, but Dangerous

The distinction was made earlier between two phases of the integrationist effort: the Possibility Question *("Can* and *Should* theology and psychology be integrated?")* and the Procedural Question *("How* are theology and psychology best integrated?")*. The two approaches discussed above involve flawed reasoning at the Possibility level. That is, they are appealed to in defense of the notion that secular psychology *can* and *should* be appealed to in order to supplement the teachings of Scripture in the attempt to best help struggling people.[86]

On two important counts, this third approach is distinct from the first two. First, this mentality operates at the level of the Procedural Question, generally *making no attempt* to address the Possibility Question (i.e., the "necessary and constituent issues" which lay below the "waterline"). Second, from the perspective of evangelical thought this construct involves no *intrinsic* fallacy of theology or logic;[87] indeed, it proceeds upon a sincere confession of a high view of inerrant Scripture characteristic of orthodox evangelical theology, it affirms the *distinctive* character and authority

---

[86] The Two-Book fallacy argues that the findings of men *can* and *should* be appealed to because they fall under the broad(ened) category of general revelation, and thus have divine sanction; that is, the argument has force because it raises the findings of men to the level of Scripture. The No-Book fallacy argues that the findings of men *can* and *should* be appealed to because, by reason of the limitations of the human interpreter of Scripture, theology can have no *greater* authority than the findings of men; in other words, this argument has force because it lowers the Scripture to the level of men's discoveries. Each argument addresses the POSSIBILITY phase of the integrationist effort; neither speaks to the PROCEDURAL phase.

[87] That is, it is valid and cogent as to logic, definition and theology *in all that it says.* The argument below is that this approach is fallacious not in what it says but in what it *assumes.*

81

of all revealed truth, and it includes an honest commitment to honor that reality in the work of constructing a model of counseling. However, it will be argued that this approach to integration *becomes fallacious* when employed in the effort to reconcile theology and *psychology*.

The Approach Identified

The Rule-Book approach may be reduced to the following propositions:

The Axiomatic Affirmation:

The Scriptures are *uniquely* and *entirely* the inerrant and authoritative Word of God.[88]

The Theological Formulation:

God has made Himself known through both General and Special Revelation. The only channel of Special Revelation available to man today is the recorded Scriptures. Thus, the only propositional and objective revelation of God available to men today is the Bible.[89]

---

[88] Not all integrationists who employ the Rule-Book approach would embrace a view of Scripture as high as this, but such a view is in fact logically necessary to the mentality. Further, a mitigated view of the character of Scripture would only compromise the integrity of the Rule-Book approach, and here that mentality is being considered in its most noble and viable expression.

[89] In fact, Rule-Book theorists handle the issue of general revelation in distinguishable ways. Often they commit the fallacy of identifying the discoveries of men, including those in the psychotherapeutic world, as belonging to that category (as in the Two-Book fallacy above). There is an intrinsic inconsistency in thus categorizing human discoveries as revelation and then

The Epistemological Conclusion:

The Bible and the Bible alone must function for the believer as the only and sufficient rule for faith and practice.

The Integrationist Ramifications:

All truth-claims which are the result of men's cogitations, investigations, and theorizing must be subjected to the Word of God which alone will be allowed to pass judgment as to the veracity and applicability of those truth-claims. The Bible and the Bible alone will be granted the role of *falsification*; that is, if a truth-claim is discerned to contradict or compromise a truth established in Scripture, that competing truth-claim is to be adjudged false.[90]

---

positing that another form of revelation (the Bible) can sit in judgment upon those discoveries. But in this discussion the commitment to employing the Scriptures as a Rule-Book which alone can sit in judgment upon truth-claims from any other source will be taken at face value.

[90] Some would strengthen the INTEGRATIONIST RAMIFICATION at this point, insisting specifically that the believer ought to do more than utilize the Bible as a falsifier, that he ought to accept only that which the Bible explicitly *affirms*. But to say that all of the Bible is truth is not to suggest that all truth is in the Bible. Thus, it is difficult to insist that only that which can be proven *true* by an appeal to Scripture ought to be accepted. (For instance, water runs downhill; the Minnesota Twins won the World Series in 1991.) Others have insisted that the Bible contains all *Truth* (upper case), and that all men can discover is *truth* (lower case). Or the distinction is made between subjective *vis a vis* objective truth, or metaphysical *vis a vis* physical truth, or between truth and facts. But such distinctions seem entirely artificial to this researcher. In fact, all truth is true, and natural man *can* discover and appreciate truth, even subjective/metaphysical truth (e.g., the soul-satisfaction which flows from self-sacrifice). Further, there does exist such truth which is not explicitly stated in the pages of Scripture (e.g., the happy effect of a devoted pet in the life of a lonely aged person). It might be argued that all really *important* metaphysical/subjective *Truth* is recorded in Scripture, and all that men can discover on their own is

In sum, this mentality accepts the Bible and the Bible only as the *Rule-Book* (thus the title used here). It posits simply that the Scriptures will "rule" on all truth-claims; they will function as the only authoritative arbiter in all epistemological questions.[91] As one apologist for this approach summarizes:

> Truth derived from the study of any segment of general revelation, whether psychology or any other field, is not as trustworthy as the truth found in the Scriptures. This is the reason that the integrationist will filter psychological truth through biblical truth and will accept only that which is not contradictory to God's special revelation.[92]

---

really of little consequence, but such a claim is untestable and after all of no real help. It is manifest that men can discover truth. But the question for the believer when he encounters truth-claims from the world is simply this: "How do I KNOW that that which has been discovered is in fact *truth*?" That question can only be refereed by the Scriptures! Further, given the fact that all that is in the Bible is true, but that not all that is true is in the Bible (for instance, you believe that water is composed of two parts hydrogen and one part oxygen, though the Bible nowhere explicitly affirms that truth), that refereeing function cannot *always* be positive ("Truth-claim A can only be judged true if affirmed in Scripture."). However, the Bible must always function negatively in a contest of ideas (that is, "If truth-claim B compromises or contradicts any verity of Scripture it must be rejected, no matter how compelling it seems to be!"). This is what is meant by the phrase, "the role of falsification." For instance, although the psychotherapeutic world insists that men suffer from a deficient view of their own importance, the Bible believer who recognizes that proposition as a contradiction of the Scriptural teaching concerning fallen man is compelled to reject the notion.

[91] Compare Robert C. Roberts, in an analysis of the counseling model of Carl Rogers: "Let me say at the outset that I consider it quite possible for pagan insights to help the church, if they are properly adapted. But we must be aggressively critical, testing the spirits, to make sure the gospel of Jesus, and the Christian life, are furthered by these pagan elements, and not hindered or contradicted by them" (*Christianity Today*, November 8, 1985, p 25).

[92] William F. English, "An Integrationist's Critique of and Challenge to

Surely this is an integrationist construct with which a believer who espouses a high view of Scripture can live! Indeed, this is the very stuff of maintaining any sort of testimony in a fallen world. Is there any aspect of life in which culture does not confront the thinking believer with theories and mores and value-systems which must be challenged Biblically? And is this Rule-Book mentality not the spirit in which that believer ought to respond to those challenges? It is my persuasion that the Rule-Book approach is precisely the mentality which ought to rule in the mind of a believer as he seeks to shine as a light in the midst of a crooked and perverse generation.

The Approach Critiqued

Why then has this mentality been denominated a "fallacy" here? Quite simply, my contention is that although the Rule-Book approach is legitimate as a basic approach to assessing the morality and veracity of the great body of the truth-claims offered by the world, it is fallacious to employ even this noble approach as a *methodology* for integration when a *rationale* in defense of the effort has not been provided. It is invalid to proceed to the Procedural

---

the Bobgan's View of Counseling and Psychotherapy" *JPT* 1990:18(3), p 229. Compare Gangel, "Integrating Faith and Learning: Principles and Process" *BibSac*, April-June, 1978, p 106, where Gangel speaks of building a Biblical/theological sieve through which to "filter" the "kinds of information which bombard [the student's] mental processes." English also uses the "filter" analogy to characterize the Rule-Book approach: "...the integrationist will filter psychological truth through biblical truth and will accept only that which is not contradictory to God's special revelation" (English, *Ibid*, p 229). Perhaps the most aggressive and commendable (though, I would argue, nonetheless flawed) attempt to articulate a functioning Rule-Book model is that of Lawrence J. Crabb, Jr. in *Understanding People* (Grand Rapids, MI: Zondervan Publishing Company, pp 25-73).

level without satisfactorily addressing the Possibility issues, *no matter the inherent merit of the construct employed at the Procedural level.*

It was stated earlier that my purpose in this article is to excite in the reader a willingness to revisit the issue of whether the integration of theology and psychology *can* or *should* be pursued. The literature would suggest that this issue of *moral rationale* is not much discussed today within the integrationist community; indeed, the existence of the rationale is the *given* upon which countless attempts are made to construct a coherent methodology of integration.

On the other hand, the one apologetic construct which *is* consistently invoked within the evangelical community of integrationists is that which appeals axiomatically to the Two-Book mentality, the notion that all of man's discoveries fall under the broad(ened) category of general revelation and thus must be acknowledged to possess the veracity and authority intrinsic to revelation. But the Two-Book approach was earlier demonstrated to be fallacious. If that is so, then the *methodological* superstructure has been deprived of its foundational *rationale.* That is, to the degree that the Rule-Book *methodology* (which dominates in the evangelical community) is dependent upon the Two-Book *rationale* (which has been demonstrated to be bankrupt), the requirements of a cogent integrationist approach have been compromised and the methodology itself is rendered suspect.

And it is for just this reason that the Rule-Book approach is here adjudged fallacious as a methodology to integrate theology and *psychology.* As indicated in the "Suggested Construct" (see the box at the beginning of this essay), it is at once foolish and dangerous to move to the Procedural Question *("How* can integration best be done?") without having satisfactorily addressed the Possibility Questions *("Can* and *should* integration be done?"). The issue reduces itself here, then, to the integrity *not* of this specific integrationist method, but of the integrationist impulse. No matter the merit of the method, if the impulse is either foolish or wicked, the effort demands to be abandoned. Frankly, it is my persuasion that the impulse is in fact both foolish and wicked!

To be sure, that sort of proposition will not be well received by many in the evangelical community. But is there not a cause? Is there not a reason to be suspicious of the presumption that either of the Possibility Questions can be answered in the affirmative? If the proposition before the evangelical house is that "The integration of Christian theology and secular psychology *can* be done!", the affirmative can be carried only if the case can be made that those two disciplines can indeed by reconciled--disciplines which were so long openly and consciously hostile to one another, which build upon sets of presuppositions so evidently mutually exclusive, and which operate within world-views so entirely foreign to one another.[93] The burden of proof is certainly upon those who would argue in the affirmative.

By the same token, if the proposition to be considered by the believing community is that "The integration of Christian theology and secular psychology *ought to* be done!", the case must be made that there is some intrinsic inadequacy or imperfection in the Scriptures which demands that insights be gleaned from secular psychology which will redress those deficiencies and enable Christian counselors to more effectively help hurting people. But the Scriptures make explicit claim to sufficiency, especially with

---

[93] An article surveying Christian counseling ministries begins with the observation that "In March 1907, Sigmund Freud took on God, presenting a paper before the Vienna Psychanalytic Society in which he concluded that religion was a `universal obsessional neurosis.' Ever after psychiatrists have seen religion as a symptom of problems, not a source of healing. No field has been more resolutely irreligious" (Tim Stafford, "Franchising Hope," *Christianity Today*, May 18, 1992, p 22).

regard to issues of fruitful living (2 Tim 3:15-17; 2 Pet 1:3). Further, for hundreds of years the Christian world has rested secure in the confidence that those Scriptures are in fact fully sufficient in all of the vicissitudes and adversities of life. Surely these realities would leave any evangelical suspicious of the suggestion that any demerit or deficiency is intrinsic to those Scriptures.[94]

It might be responded that if the methodology is adequate (i.e., if the Rule-Book mentality genuinely and adequately honors the unique character of Scripture) it will suffice even if the Possibility issues have not been addressed. Again one might anticipate that if theology and psychology were indeed ontologically irreconcilable they would demonstrate themselves so in the effort to integrate them. But such a supposition is born of spiritual naiveté. In fact, there are some discomfiting moral realities which must be factored into this question: the reality that many of the notions of secular psychology, though contrary to Scripture, are nonetheless seductively attractive to the Adamic nature (e.g., the tendency to make victims of virtually everyone, thus relieving them of moral responsibility for sin); the reality that if the Christian psychotherapist accepts the validity of secular psychology he makes available to himself professional status and affluence that he almost certainly could not have known otherwise; the reality that even armed with the Rule-Book methodology many integrationists have embraced concepts which seem manifestly contrary to the plain teachings of Scripture.[95] These realities

---

[94] A careful and extensive defense of the notion of the sufficiency of Scripture is to be found in *Our Sufficiency in Christ*, John MacArthur (Dallas: Word Publishing, 1991). See especially "Truth in a World of Theory" (pp 73ff.).

[95] See for instance John E. Wagner, "National Association of

remind us that the injunction of the apostle that believers "make no provision for the flesh in regard to its lusts" (Rom 13:14) does have application to this issue.

In sum, it is acknowledged that from the standpoint of one who confesses a high view of Scripture and who seeks to implement a thorough-going Biblicist world-view, the Rule-Book mentality is an airtight integrationist methodology. But I have alleged that in the effort to integrate theology and psychology, that methodology has been employed imprudently and recklessly; my fear is that the damage done to the cause of authentic New Testament Christianity has been beyond measure. That indictment of recklessness arises from the observation that the effort has proceeded to the methodological phase without adequately addressing the issue of rationale. All would acknowledge that there is no virtue in doing well a task which is either foolish or wicked. If the attempt to integrate Christian theology with secular psychology is *neither* foolish *nor* wicked, then my criticism here is entirely off the mark. But because the evangelical integrationist community has not adequately addressed the epistemological issues "below the waterline," that effort has not been *proven* either wise or virtuous. Christian integrationists owe it to themselves, to their colleagues, to their patients, and to their Lord to produce a cogent and exegetically sound rationale for the impulse *before* they proceed to the matter of method.

Conclusion

The tenor of this article has been almost entirely--perhaps, disturbingly--negative. I have examined three (sometimes overlapping) approaches currently utilized in the effort to integrate

---

Evangelicals: Amplifying His Voice," *Christianity Today*, May 9, 1975, pp 45ff.

secular psychology and orthodox evangelical theology. First the Two-Book approach was considered, which broadens the category of general revelation to include all those data which result from man's investigation into the created order, thus imbuing the perceived realities of secular psychology with the status and authority of revelation; that approach was assessed as confused in its definitions and thus destructive of the authoritative role which evangelical theology has assigned to Scripture alone. Second, the No-Book mentality was analyzed, the approach which presupposes that the limitations and preconditioning common to all human beings so cripple their ability to access even an authoritative and dependable truth-source such as Scripture that theology itself can be no more dependable than any other source of knowledge; that mentality was characterized as corrupt in its theological presuppositions and conclusions, and as dishonest in its estimation of the character of Scripture. Finally, focus was upon the Rule-Book approach, which honors Scripture as the only authoritative propositional truth-source available today, and which acknowledges that the Scriptures alone must be granted the role of falsification in every contest of competing truth-claims to which they speak; that approach was recognized as commendable, with the caveat that even such a laudable approach should not be employed until it is established that the integration of psychology and theology is itself a virtuous and wise effort.

     And yet, even in the face of this negative assessment of so much of what is going on in the world of Christian psychology, God forbid that this article would leave the reader with a sense of loss or despair. Even if these criticisms are valid, if secular psychology is in fact a "broken cistern that can hold no water," Christian counselors are in so sense impoverished. We simply need to be reminded that it is foolish to "forsake the fountain of living waters" which is to be found in the Word of God. In a word, the Scriptures are sufficient.

Almost twenty years ago, in an article in which he was exploring the dynamics of an integrationist construct which would honor the unique character of Scripture, J. Robertson McQuilkin addressed the question, "To what extent do the behavioral sciences among Evangelicals give evidence of being under the authority of Scripture?" In developing an answer to that pivotal issue, he issued a very sobering warning:

> ...the range of success in integrating truth derived empirically and truth revealed in Scripture (and, indeed, the interest in making such an integration) varies so widely in evangelical circles that no precise answer to my question is possible. Nevertheless it is very important to raise the question because the potential for good or evil is so great. A resounding affirmative should be possible: "The great majority of evangelical scholars in the behavioral sciences give consistent evidence of thorough integration with Scripture in control." If such an affirmation cannot be made with confidence, we are in great danger because of the pervasive power of humanistic thinking in our society and because of the subtlety with which Scripture's authority is eroded.
>
> My thesis is that in the next two decades the greatest threat to Biblical authority is the behavioral scientist who would in all good conscience man the barricades to defend the front door against any theologian who would attack the inspiration and authority of Scripture while all the while

himself smuggling the content of Scripture out the back door through cultural or psychological interpretation.[96]

McQuilkin then catalogued several examples of "cultural or psychological interpretation" which were being accepted by the Christian psychological community at that time, but which reflect a weak view of the authority of Scripture (skepticism toward the grammatical-historical interpretation of Scripture; denial of the moral wickedness of homosexuality; a genre of Christian literature instructing readers how to lead fruitful lives but making no appeal to the standard Christian graces nor to the power of the Holy Spirit; recommendation of cathartic ventilation at the expense of the virtue of self-control; the claim that a knowledge of the Gospel is unnecessary to salvation), after which he concludes, "...we are in great danger of the wide-scale subversion of Biblical authority by those who are committed to that authority on the conscious and theoretical level, but who through uncritical use of behavioral scientific methodology have unwittingly come under its control."[97]

---

[96] J. Robertson McQuilkin, "The Behavioral Sciences under the Authority of Scripture," *Journal of the Evangelical Theological Society* March, 1977:20(1), p 37.

[97] Ibid, p 41. McQuilkin struggles to define a strategy to protect evangelicalism from this tendency. He recommends that Scripture be in "functional control" over the theories and methods devised by the psychotherapist, an attitude which involves "not just mental assent to the thesis, which would make for theoretical or constitutional control, but acute awareness of the danger involved and a jealous commitment to the Bible first and last as the originating and controlling source of ideas about man and his relationships" (p 42). He suggests that one practical step to insure that control the Christian behavioral scientist also be trained in theology (p 43). This is interesting in contrast to James R. Beck, "The Role of Theology in the Training of Christian Psychologists" *JPT* 1992:20(2), pp 99-109, in which Beck seeks to define some sort of an apologetic for the idea of thus including theological training. He posits

That warning was issued in 1977. McQuilkin's fear was for "the next two decades." The evangelical community may be ahead of schedule!

"three major roles theology can play in the training curriculum for Christian psychologists," and in developing the second of those he states, "When our quest for understanding thus leads us to the limits of psychology's ability to explain, the Christian can utilize theological understanding to help guide the ongoing search" (p 103). Rather a long way from McQuilkin's "jealous commitment to the Bible first and last as the originating and controlling source of ideas about man and his relationships"!

Chapter 3

The Sufficiency of Scripture to Diagnose and Cure Souls
Dr. David Powlison

How do destructive people become constructive? How do out-of-control people become fruitfully self-controlled? How do rigid people become flexible? How do drifty people learn focus? How do hopeless people grow in hope? How do angry people learn to make peace? And even before we can ask How? we must ask, Why are troubled people troubled? What's wrong with us?

In modern society, Scripture's way of explaining and engaging people has been largely displaced. What must be done to recover the centrality of Scripture for helping people to grow up into the image of Christ? How can face-to-face "helping" relationships be reconfigured to serve as instruments of the only enduring wisdom and the only true humanity?

To recover the centrality of Scripture for the cure of souls demands two things: *conviction* backed up with *content*. The conviction? Scripture is about understanding and helping people. The scope of Scripture's sufficiency includes those face-to-face relationships that our culture labels "counseling" or "psychotherapy." The content? The problems, needs, and struggles of real people—right down to the details—must be rationally explained by the categories with which the Bible teaches us to understand human life.

Conviction alone simply waves a flag and eventually degrades into sloganeering. But convictions demonstrated in action, convictions shown to be penetrating, comprehensive, and subtle, will edify the teachable and even persuade the skeptical. The church needs persuading that the conviction is true. A key ingredient in such persuasion will be to parade the riches of Scripture for curing souls.

In the pages that follow, we will look first at the *conviction* that Scripture is about "problems in living." We will then explore one small bit of content, the term, "lusts of the flesh." This phrase is central to how God explains us. It cuts to the root of our problems in living, but it has languished in near uselessness.

Conviction: Systematic Biblical Counseling

What is a genuinely biblical view of the problems of the human soul and the procedures of ministering grace? Such a view must establish a number of things. First, we must ask, does Scripture give us the materials and call to construct something that might fairly be called "systematic biblical counseling." In fact, we do have the goods for a coherent and comprehensive practical theology of face-to-face ministry. Scripture is dense with explanations, with instructions, with implications. We have much work to do to understand and to articulate the biblical "model." But we don't have to make it up or borrow from models that others have made up as ways to explain people.

In many places, the Holy Spirit reflects on the sufficiency of the treasure that He has created through His prophets and apostles. For example, in one classic passage Scripture proclaims itself as that which makes us "wise unto salvation." This is a comprehensive description of transforming human life from all that ails us (2 Tim. 3:15-17). This same passage goes on to speak of the Spirit's words as purposing to teach us. The utter simplicity and unsearchable complexity of Scripture enlightens us about God, about ourselves, about good and evil, true and false, grace and judgment, about the world that surrounds us with its many forms of suffering and beguilement, with its opportunities to shed light into darkness. Through such teaching, riveted to particular people in particular situations, God *exposes* in specific detail what is wrong with human life. No deeper or truer or better analysis of the human condition can be concocted. God's words reconstruct and transform what they define as defective. He speaks as He acts, to *straighten out* wrongs through the corrective power of grace. To promote any solution but God's is to offer opiates to the masses, the stuff of dreams, not the stuff of real answers for real problems. And this God continues to personalize what is true, performing His wisdom-renewing work in an ongoing process. The net result? We begin to live like Jesus Christ Himself.

Scripture accomplishes our renewal in the image of Him who is wisdom incarnate, so that we become equipped for every good work. Biblical teaching addresses countless topics. One crucial topic is the area of human motivation—the interpretation and evaluation of our desires. The Bible's view of what is disordered in human motivation sharply challenges all secular pretenders to explanatory wisdom about why we do what we do.

Content: "Lusts of the Flesh," A Case Study in Systematic Practical Theology

The simplest way to discover why a person does, says, thinks, or feels certain things is to ask, "What do you *want*? What *desires* made him do that? What *yearning* led her to say that? What *longings* animate me when I follow that train of thoughts and fantasy? What did they *fear* when they felt so anxious?"[98] Such questions are plain common sense. Abraham Maslow sensibly described matters this way:

---

[98] A fear is simply desire turned on its head: "I don't want."

The original criterion of motivation and the one that is still used by all human beings... is the subjective one. I am motivated when I feel desire or want or yearning or wish or lack.[99]

So, pose the question, "What do you want?" to yourself and others. Then pay attention to the answers. If you listen to people, they'll often tell you exactly what they want. "I got angry because she dissed me, and I want respect." "She became tongue-tied because she yearns for acceptance." "He feels anxious because money's tight, and he fears that poverty will prove he's a failure." "Those fantasies of heroism and success play in my mind because I long to be important." Even when a person is inarticulate or unaware, you can often deduce the answer with a high degree of accuracy if you watch and listen closely, and if you know yourself well. Part of knowing any person well is learning what he or she typically lives for—the pattern of desires.

The Meaning of Our Desires

But naming what you want is the easy part. The harder part is this: how should you now *interpret* what you've identified? Naming is not the same as understanding what your wants mean and how you should evaluate them. The meaning of our desires is not common sense at all. Instead, it's a battleground for contending theories of human nature, competing interpretations of the underlying dynamics of human psychology. Abraham Maslow, for example, went on to explain our desires this way:

---

[99] Abraham Maslow, *Toward a Psychology of Being*, 2nd ed. (New York: Van Nostrand Reinhold, 1968), 22.

It is these needs which are essentially deficits in the organism, empty holes, so to speak, which must be filled up for health's sake, and furthermore must be filled from without by human beings *other* than the subject, that I shall call deficits or deficiency needs.[100]

Is it true that we have these "needs" for respect, acceptance, money, or significance that must be met from outside? Many other great psychologists—B. F. Skinner, Alfred Adler, Sigmund Freud, Victor Frankl, Aaron Beck, Carl Jung, and Virginia Satir, to name a few—didn't think so at all. They disagreed fiercely with each other, too!

The God who reveals His way of thinking in the Bible doesn't agree either with Maslow or with any of the others. In fact, no one ever rightly understands and weighs desires without God's self-revelation in Scripture. Neither lowbrow common sense nor highbrow personality theory gets it straight. God must show us how to properly interpret our wants, because we are compulsive misinterpreters: we don't want the true interpretation. It's too threatening to the pursuit of God-less autonomy that is our deepest, darkest, most persistent, and most inadmissible passion.

God's Interpretation and Intervention

"What do you crave, want, pursue, wish, long for, hope to get, feel you need, or passionately desire?" God has an interpretation of this that cuts to the marrow of who you are and what you live for. He sees our hearts as an embattled kingdom ruled either by one kind of desire or by another kind. On the one hand, what *lusts of the flesh* hijack your heart from God's rule? On

---

[100] Ibid., 22-23.

the other hand, what holy *passions* express your love for God?" Our desires are not a given, but a fundamental choice. Desires are most often unruly, disorderly, inordinate affections for XYZ, a good thing that I insanely need. Sometimes they are natural affections for xyz, made sane and orderly by subordination to passionate love for God that claims my heart, soul, mind, and might. Our desires are often idolatrous cravings to get good gifts (overthrowing or ignoring the Giver). Sometimes they are intense desires for the Giver Himself as supremely more important than whatever good gifts we might gain or lose from His hand. That's the first unique thing God shows us about human psychology. This cosmic battleground is something none of the secular psychologists have seen or can see, because they can't see that deeply into why we do what we do. Their own motives give them reasons not to want to see that deeply and honestly. It would mean admitting sin.

To examine desires is one of the most fruitful ways to come at the topic of motivation biblically. New Testament authors repeatedly allude to life-controlling cravings when they summarize the innermost dynamics of the human soul. Which will triumph, the natural deviancy of the lusts of the flesh or the restored sanity of the desires of the Spirit? Christ's apostles have the greatest confidence that only the resources of the gospel of grace and truth possess sufficient depth and power to change us in the ways we most need changing. The mercies of God work to *forgive* and then to *change* what is deeply evil, but even more deeply curable by God's hand and voice. The inworking power of grace qualitatively transforms the very desires that psychologists assume are hardwired, unchangeable, morally neutral givens. Christ's grace slays and replaces (in a lifelong battle) the very lusts that the theories variously explain as "needs" or "drives" or "instincts" or "goals." That's the second unique thing God shows us about human psychology. We can be fundamentally rewired by the merciful presence of the Messiah. None of the secular psychologists say this or can say this. They have no power to address us so deeply, and they don't want to address us at the level of what we (and they) live for. It would mean confessing Christ.

We will use a series of fifteen questions to probe the world of our desires.

1. What is the most common way that the New Testament talks about what's wrong with people?

Lusts of the flesh (cravings or pleasures) is a summary term for what is wrong with us in God's eyes. In sin, people turn *from* God to serve what they want. By grace, people turn to God from their cravings. According to the Lord's assessment, we all formerly lived in the lusts of our flesh, indulging the desires of the flesh and the mind (Eph. 2:3). Those outside of Christ are thoroughly controlled by what they want. ("Of course I live for money, reputation, success, looks, and love. What else is there to live for?") And the most significant inner conflict in Christians is between what the Spirit wants and what we want.

But the term "lust" has become almost useless to modern readers of the Bible. It is reduced to sexual desire. Take a poll of the people in your church, asking them the meaning of "lusts of the flesh." Sex will appear first on every list! Greed, pride, gluttonous craving, or mammon worship might be added in the answers of a few of the more thoughtful believers. But the subtleties and details get washed out, and a crucial biblical term for explaining human life languishes. In contrast, the New Testament writers use this term as a comprehensive category for the human dilemma! It will pay us to think carefully about its manifold meanings. We need to expand our understanding of a term that has been truncated and drained of significance. We need to learn to see life through these lenses, and to use these categories skillfully.

The New Testament repeatedly focuses on the "lusts of the flesh" as a summary of what is wrong with the human heart that underlies bad behavior. For example, 1 John 2:16 contrasts the love of the Father with "all that is in the world, the lust of the flesh and the lust of the eyes and the boastful pride of life."[101] This does not mean that the New Testament is internalistic.[102] In each of these passages, behavior intimately connects to motive, and motive to behavior. Wise counselors follow the model of Scripture and move back and forth between lusts of the flesh and the tangible works of the flesh, between faith and the tangible fruit of the Spirit.

---

[101] See also Rom. 13:14; Gal. 5:16-17; Eph. 2:2 and 4:22; James 1:14-15; 4:1-3; 1 Peter 1:14; 2 Peter 1:4. The Old Testament typically focuses on idolatry as the way people go astray. This doesn't mean that the Old Testament is externalistic. Visible idolatry simply registers, for all to see, the failure to love the Lord God with heart, soul, mind, and might; it registers an internal defection. There are places where the problem of idolatry is turned into a metaphor for the most basic internalized sin (e.g., Ezek. 14), and visible idolatry always expressed a defection of heart from God. There are places where the human heart is described as insane (Eccl. 9:3), evil (Gen. 6:5), full of cravings and lies (Num. 11-25), uncircumcised, hard, blind, and so forth. The New Testament also equates sinful desires with idolatry, metaphorically, on several occasions (e.g., Col. 3:5; Eph. 5:5). Idolatry can summarize every false, lifecontrolling master (1 John 5:21).

[102] We often hear warnings against externalistic religion. But internalistic religion creates equally serious problems. Christians often seek some experience or feeling, some sense of total brokenness, some comprehensive inward transformation – and miss that biblical change is practical and progressive, inside and out.

2. Why do people do specific ungodly things?

Lusts of the flesh answers the WHY question operating at the heart of any system attempting to explain human behavior. Specific ruling desires—lusts, cravings or pleasures—create bad fruit. Inordinate desires explain and organize diverse bad behavior and mental processes: words, actions, emotions, thoughts, plans, attitudes, brooding memories, fantasies. James 1:13-16 establishes this intimate and pervasive connection between motive and fruit this way:

> Let no one say when he is tempted, "I am being tempted by God"; for God cannot be tempted by evil, and He Himself does not tempt anyone. But each one is tempted when he is carried away and enticed by his own lust. Then when lust has conceived, it gives birth to sin; and when sin is accomplished, it brings forth death. Do not be deceived, my beloved brethren.[103]

In modern language such sinful cravings often masquerade as expectations, goals, felt needs, wishes, demands, longings, drives, and so forth. People talk about their motives in ways that anesthetize themselves and others to the true significance of what they are describing.

3. But what's wrong with wanting things that seem good?

What makes our desires wrong? This question becomes particularly perplexing to people when the object of their desires is

---

[103] See also Gal. 5:16-6:10; James 1:13-16; James 3:14-4:12.

a good thing. Notice some of the adjectives that get appended to our cravings: *evil, polluted* lusts.[104] What do such strong words describe? Sometimes the object of desire itself is evil: e.g., to kill someone, to steal, to control the cocaine trade on the Eastern seaboard. But often the object of our desire is good, and the evil lies in the lordship of the desire. Our will replaces God's as that which determines how we live. John Calvin put it this way: "We teach that all human desires are evil, and charge them with sin— not in that they are natural, but because they are inordinate."[105] In other words, the evil in our desires often lies not in what we want but in the fact that we want it too much. Natural affections (for any good thing) become inordinate, ruling cravings. We are meant to be ruled by godly passions and desires (see Question 15, below). Natural desires for good things are meant to exist subordinate to our desire to please the Giver of gifts. Grasping that the evil lies in the ruling status of the desire, not the object, is frequently a turning point in selfunderstanding, in seeing the need for Christ's mercies, and in changing.

Consider this example. A woman commits adultery, then repents. She and her husband rebuild their marriage, painstakingly, patiently. Eight months later the man finds himself plagued with subtle suspiciousness and irritability. The wife senses it and feels a bit like she lives under FBI surveillance. The husband is grieved by his suspiciousness because he has no objective reasons for it. "I've forgiven her; we've rebuilt our marriage; we've never communicated better; why do I hold on to this mistrust?" It emerges that he is willing to forgive the past, but he attempts to control the future. His craving could be stated this way: "I want to

---

[104] Col. 3:5; 2 Peter 2:10.

[105] John Calvin, Institutes of the Christian Religion, translated by Ford Lewis Battles, (Philadelphia: Westminster Press), 604.

guarantee that betrayal never, ever happens again." The object of desire is good; its ruling status poisons his ability to love. The lust to ensure her fidelity places him in the stance of continually evaluating and judging his wife, rather than loving her. What he wants cannot be guaranteed this side of heaven. He sees the point, sees his inordinate desire to ensure his marital future. But he bursts out, "What's wrong with wanting my wife to love me? What's wrong with wanting her to remain faithful to our marriage?" Here is where this truth is so sweet. There is nothing wrong with the object of desire; there is everything wrong when it rules his life. The process of restoring that marriage took a long step forward as he took this to heart.

Are preferences, wishes, desires, longings, hopes, and expectations always sinful then? Of course not. What theologians used to call "natural affections" are part of our humanity. They are part of what makes humans different from stones, able to tell the difference between blessing and curse, pleasure and pain. It is right that we don't want the pains of rejection, death, poverty, and illness, and we do want the joys of friendship, life, money, and health. Jesus was no masochist; of course He cried out, "Let this cup pass from Me!" The moral issue always turns on whether the desire takes on a ruling status. If it does, it will produce visible sins: anger, grumbling, immorality, despair, what James so vividly termed "disorder and every evil thing" (James 3:16). Jesus was no idolater; He entrusted Himself to His Father and obeyed. "Nevertheless, not My will but Yours be done." But Jesus was also no stoic or Buddhist aiming to flat-line human desires. His desires were strong, but mastered by love for His Father. If natural affections remain submitted to God, such faith will produce visible love. For example, if you wish your son or daughter to grow up to be a Christian, and your child strays, it may break your heart, but it will not make you sin against either God or your child. Anger, obsessive anxiety, suspiciousness, or manipulation gives evidence that desire for a good thing has grown monstrous. Wise parenting demonstrates that the desire, a passionate and broken-hearted love, is aligned rightly.

4. Why don't people see this as the problem?

Consider a second adjective that Scripture attaches to the phrase "lusts of the flesh": *deceitful* lusts.[106] Our desires deceive us because they present themselves as so plausible. When natural affections become warped and monstrous, they blind us. Who wouldn't want good health, financial comfort, a loving spouse, good kids, success on the job, kind parents, tasty food, a life without traffic jams, control over circumstances? Yet cravings for these things lead to every sort of evil. The things people desire are delightful as blessings received from God, but terrible as rulers. They make good goods but bad gods. They beguile, promising blessing, but delivering sin and death.

Some sins are high-handed, done with full awareness of choice (Ps.19:13). Other sins reflect the blind, dark, habitual, compulsive, hardened, ignorant, confused, instinctive insanity of sin.[107] One of the joys of biblical ministry comes when you are able to help turn on the lights in another person's dark room.

People usually don't see their desires as lusts. Our souls awaken as the light of God's analytic gaze disturbs our ignorance and self-deceit. Souls are then comforted and cured by the love that shed substitutionary blood to purchase the inexpressible gift.

---

[106] Eph. 4:22

[107] Gen. 6:5; Ps. 19:12; Eccl. 9:3; Jer. 17:9; Eph. 4:17-22; 1 Tim. 1:13; 2 Peter 2:10-22.

I have yet to meet a couple locked in hostility (and the accompanying fear, self-pity, hurt, self-righteousness) who really understood and reckoned with their motives. James 4:1-3 teaches that cravings underlie conflicts. Why do you fight? It's not "because my wife/husband…"—it's because of something about you. Couples who see what rules them— cravings for affection, attention, power, vindication, control, comfort, a hassle-free life— can repent and find God's grace made real to them and then learn how to make peace.

5. Is the phrase "lusts of the flesh" useful in practical life and counseling?

Apply the term to twentieth-century experience, redeeming the evasive language people substitute. People frequently talk about what they want, expect, wish for, desire, demand, need, long for. Pop psychologies typically validate these needs and longings as neutral givens. Little do people realize that much of the time they are actually describing sinful usurpers of God's rule over their lives: inordinate desires, lusts of the flesh, cravings. They are being honest about what they want, but they aren't interpreting their experience rightly. For example, listen to children talk when they are angry, disappointed, demanding, contrary: "But I want. . . . But I don't want. . . ." In our family we began teaching our children about the "I-wantsies" before they were two years old. We wanted them to grasp that sin was more than behavior. For example, analyze any argument or outburst of anger and you will find ruling expectations and desires that are being frustrated (James 4:1-2). The language people typically use day-to-day gets you into the details of a person's life, but it usually comes with a distorted interpretation attached. Wise counseling must reinterpret that experience into biblical categories, taking the more pointed reality

106

of "lusts, cravings, pleasures" and mapping it onto the "felt needs" that underlie much sin and misery. The very unfamiliarity of the phrase is an advantage, if you explain it carefully and show its relevance and applicability. Behavioral sins demand a horizontal resolution—as well as vertical repentance. But motivational sins have first and foremost to do with God. Repentance quickens the awareness of relationship with the God of grace.

6. Does each person have one "root sin"?

With good reason, the Bible usually refers to the *lusts* (plural) of the flesh. The human heart can generate a lust tailored to any situation. Again John Calvin powerfully described how cravings "boil up" within us, how the mind of man is a "factory of idols."[108] We are infested with lusts. Listen closely to any person given to complaining, and you will observe the creativity of our cravings. Certainly one particular craving may so frequently appear that it seems to be a "root sin": love of mammon, fear of man and craving for approval, love of preeminence or control, desire for pleasure, and so forth, can dictate much of life! But all people have all the typical cravings.

Realizing the diversity in human lusts gives great flexibility and penetration to counseling. For example, one lust can generate very diverse sins, as 1 Timothy 6:10 states: "The love of money is a root of all sorts of evil." Every one of the Ten Commandments, and more, can be broken by someone who loves and serves money.

The craving for money and material possessions is an organizing theme for symptomatic sins as diverse as anxiety, theft, compulsive shopping, murder, jealousy, marital discord, a sense of inferiority or of superiority compared to others, sexual immorality

---

[108] John Calvin, *Institutes of the Christian Religion*, 65, 108.

that trades sex for material advantage, and so forth. On the flip side, a single behavioral sin can emerge from very different lusts. For example, sexual immorality might occur for many different reasons: erotic pleasure, financial advantage, revenge on a spouse or parent, fear of saying no to an authority, pursuit of approval, enjoyment of power over another's sexual response, the quest for social status or career advancement, pity for someone and playing the savior, fear of losing a potential marriage partner, escape from boredom, peer pressure, and so forth! Wise biblical counselors dig for specifics. They don't assume all people have the same characteristic flesh, or that a person always does a certain thing for the same reasons. The flesh is creative in iniquity.

7. How can you tell if a desire is inordinate rather than natural?

By their *fruits* you know them. Human motivation is not a theoretical mystery; there is no need to engage in a long, introspective archeological dig. Evil desires produce bad fruits that can be seen, heard, and felt (James 1:15; 3:16). For example, a father who wants his child to grow up to become a Christian reveals the status of that desire by whether he is a good father or is manipulative, fearful, angry, and suspicious. In a good father, the desire is subordinate to God's will that he love his child. In a sinful father, the desire rules and produces moral and emotional chaos. Similarly, a wife who wants to be loved reveals the status of that desire by whether or not she loves and respects her husband. Visible fruit reveals whether God rules or a lust rules.

It is a serious mistake to engage in introspective "idol hunts," attempting to dig out and weigh every kink in the human soul. The Bible calls for a more straightforward form of self-examination: an outburst of anger invites reflection on what craving ruled the heart, so that we might repent intelligently. The Bible's purposes are "extraspective," not introspective: to move out toward God in repentant faith (James 4:6-10) and then to move out towards the one wronged by anger, making peace in repentance, humility, and love.

8. Is it even right to talk about the heart, since the Bible teaches that the heart is unknowable to anyone but God? (1 Sam. 16:7; Jer. 17:9)

No one but God can *see, explain, control* or *change* another person's heart and its choices. There is no underlying reason why a person serves a particular lust rather than God; sin is irrational and insane. And there is no counseling technique that can fundamentally change hearts. But the Bible teaches us that we can *describe* what rules the heart and speak truth that God uses to convict and liberate. Effective biblical ministry probes and addresses why people do things, as well as what they do. Jesus' ministry continually exposed and challenged what people lived for, offering Himself as the only worthy ruler of the heart.

For example, 1 Samuel 16:7 says that man judges by externals while God judges the heart. Yet a few verses earlier, we are told that Saul visibly disobeyed God for a reason: he feared the people and listened to their voice, instead of fearing God and listening to Him (1 Sam. 15:24). His motives are describable, even if inexplicable. There is no deeper cause for sin than sin. Jeremiah 17:9 says that the human heart is deceitful and incomprehensible to any but God, but the same passage describes how behavior reveals that people trust in idols, themselves, and others, instead of trusting in God (Jer. 17:1-8). Scripture is frank to tell us the causes of behavior: interpersonal conflicts, for example, arise because of lusts (James 4:1-2). If anger and conflict come from a lust, the next and obvious question is, "What do you want that now rules you?"

To search out motives demands no subtle psychotherapeutic technique. People can often tell you what they want. The Israelites grumbled—a capital crime—when they had to subsist on boring food. Why? They craved flavor: fish, cucumbers, melons, leeks, onions, and garlic (Num. 11:5). Later they grumbled when they got thirsty and no oasis appeared.

Why? They craved juicy foods, or foods that demanded irrigation: grain, figs, vines, pomegranates, and water (Num. 20:5). In each case the craving reflected their apostasy from God and expressed itself in visible, audible sins. When we see the God-substitutes that claim our affections, then we see how good and necessary the grace of Jesus is in subduing hijackers and retaking the controls.

9. Doesn't the word lusts properly apply only to bodily appetites: the pleasures and comforts of sex, food, drink, rest, exercise, health?

People follow the *desires of body and mind* (Eph. 2:3). Bodily appetites—the organism's hedonistic instinct to feel good—certainly can prove powerful masters unto sin. But desires of the mind—for power, human approval, success, preeminence, wealth, self-righteousness, and so forth—are equally potent masters. The desires of the mind often present the most subtle and deceitful lusts because their outworkings are not always obvious. They don't reside in the body, but the Bible still views them as "lusts."

10. Can desires be habitual?

Paul describes a *former manner of life* characterized by deceitful lusts. Peter tells his readers not to be conformed to their *former desires*.[109] Like all other aspects of sin—beliefs, attitudes, words, deeds, emotions, thoughts, fantasies—desires can be habitual, or typical. You will counsel people who typically and repeatedly seek to control others, or to indulge in the pleasures of sloth, or to be seen as superior, or to be liked. Jesus' call to die daily to self recognizes the inertia of sin. God is in the business of creating new habitual desires, for example, an active concern for the well being of others before God.

Many counseling systems are obsessed with locating the reasons for current problems in the distant past. The Bible's worldview is much more straightforward. Sin emerges from within the person. The fact that a pattern of craving became established many years before—even that it was forged in a particular context, perhaps influenced by bad models or by experiences of being sinned against—only describes what happened and when. The past does not explain why. For example, past rejections do not cause a craving to be accepted by others, any more than current rejections cause that craving. A person who was always accepted by significant others can be just as mastered by the lust for acceptance! The occasions of a lust are never its cause. Temptations and sufferings do push our buttons, but they don't create those buttons. That brings huge hope for change in the present by the grace of God.

---

[109] Eph. 4:22, (cf. 4:17-19, which reinforces the notion of a characteristic lifestyle); 1 Peter 1:14.

11. What about fears? They seem as important in human motivation as cravings.

Fear and desire are two sides of a single coin. A sinful fear is a craving for something *not* to happen. If I want money, I fear poverty. If I long to be accepted, I'm terrified of rejection. If I fear pain or hardship, I crave comfort or pleasure. If I crave preeminence, I fear being inferior to others. With some people the fear may be more gripping and pronounced than the corresponding desire. Wise counseling will work with what is pronounced. For example, a person who grew up during the Great Depression might manifest mammon worship through a fear of poverty that shows up in anxiety, hoarding, repeated calculations of financial worth, and so forth. A wealthy thirty-something entrepreneur might manifest mammon worship through unchecked consumer spending. With the former, address fear; with the latter, address greed. They are complementary expressions of craving treasure on earth.

12. Do people ever have conflicting motives?

Certainly. The conflict between sinful lusts and the Holy Spirit's desires is a given of the Christian life (Gal. 5:16-17). All of us often have mixed motives, some good, and some bad. Most preachers and counselors will acknowledge that genuine love for Christ and people battles with perverse love for personal success and human approval.

In other instances, two sinful cravings may conflict. For example, a businessman might want to steal something from a convenience store, but holds back in fear of what people would think if they found out. In this example, mammon worship and social approval present themselves as options for the flesh; the heart inclines to the latter. People often prioritize their cravings, and arrange the priorities differently in different situations. For example, the man who would never shoplift because of the social consequences might cheat on his taxes because he's not likely to get caught, and no one who "matters" would know if he did. In this case self-will and mammon worship seize the steering wheel, and social approval moves to the back seat. The "broad way" has a thousand creative variants!

13. How does thinking about lusts relate to other ways of talking about sin, such as "sin nature," "self," "pride," "autonomy," "unbelief," and "self-centeredness"?

These words are general terms that summarize the problem of sin. One of the beauties of identifying ruling desires is that they are so specific. Insight can therefore enable more specific repentance and specific change. For example, a person who becomes angry in a traffic jam may later say, "I know my anger is sin, and it comes from self." That is true as far as it goes. But it helps to take self-knowledge a step further: "I cursed in anger because I craved to get to my appointment on time, I feared criticism from the person waiting for me, and I feared losing the profits from that sale." Repentance and change can become more specific when the person identifies these three lusts that expressed the lordship of "self" in this particular incident.

The Bible discusses sin in an astonishing variety of ways. Sometimes Scripture addresses sin at the general level: e.g., Luke 9:23-26 on "self," or Proverbs on the "fool." At other times, Scripture increases the microscope's power and treats a particular theme of sin: e.g., Philippians 3 on the pursuit of self-righteousness, or 1 Timothy 6:5-19 on love of money, or 2 Timothy 3:4 on love of pleasure. In still other places, the Bible speaks of "desires" that lead

113

to sin without specifying. This invites us to make the specific application to ourselves.[110] We could diagram this roughly as follows: (1) general terms, (2) mid-level typical patterns, and (3) detail-level specifics. (See figure 1.)

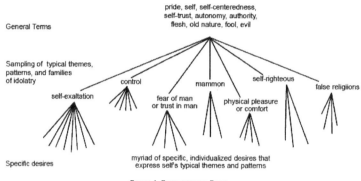

FIGURE 1. DESIRES OF THE FLESH

14. In counseling, do you just confront a person with his sinful cravings?

Wise counselors don't "just confront" anything. They do many different things to make confrontation timely and effective. Counselors never see the heart, only the evidences, so a certain tentativeness is appropriate when discussing motives. Perhaps it would be more accurate to say that counseling aims to illuminate the heart. We want to help people see themselves as they are in God's eyes, and in that to make the love of God a sweet necessity. Since counselors have the same package of typical lusts, we meet on common ground in our need for grace because of pride, fear of man, unbelief, and love of comfort and control.

---

[110] See James 1:15-15 and 4:1-2; Gal. 5:16-21; Rom. 13:12-14.

114

We can and must tackle such issues. As we saw earlier, Second Timothy 3:16 begins with "teaching." Good teaching (for example, on how Galatians 5 and James 1 connect outward sins to inward cravings) helps people examine and see themselves. Good teaching invites self-knowledge and self-confrontation. Experience with people will make you "case wise" to typical connections (e.g., the varied motives for immorality mentioned above in Question 6). Probing questions—"What did you want or expect or fear when you blew up at your wife?"—help a person reveal his ruling lusts to himself and to the counselor.

In the light of self-knowledge before God's face (Heb. 4:12-13), the Gospel offers many promises: mercy, help, the Shepherd's care in progressive sanctification (Heb. 4:14-16). "The unfolding of Your words brings light" (Ps. 119:130). Repentance, faith, and obedience become vigorous and intelligent when we see both our inner cravings and our outward sins in light of God's mercies. Work hard and carefully both on motivation issues (Romans 13:14: the lusts of the flesh versus putting on Jesus Christ) and on behavioral issues (Romans 13:12-13: the varied deeds of darkness versus proper "daylight" behavior).

The patterns, themes, or tendencies of the heart do not typically yield to a once-for-all repentance. Try dealing one mortal blow to your pride, fear of man, love of pleasure, or desire to control your world, and you will realize why Jesus spoke Luke 9:23! But genuine progress will occur where the Holy Spirit is at work. Understanding your motivational sins gives you a sense for the "themes" of your story, how your Father is at work in you over the long haul.

15. Can you change what you want?

Yes and Amen! This is central to the work of the Holy Spirit. You will always desire, love, trust, believe, fear, obey, long for, value, pursue, hope, and serve *something*. You are motivated when you feel desire. God does not anesthetize us; He redirects our desires. The Holy Spirit works to change the configuration and status of our desires, as He leads us with an intimate hand.[111] The desires of the heart are not unchangeable. God never promises to give you what you want, to meet your felt needs and longings. He tells you to be ruled by other, different desires. This is radical. God promises to change what you really want! God insists that He be first, and all lesser loves be radically subordinate.

The best way to understand this is to think about prayer. Prayer means asking. You ask because you *want* something. You ask God because you believe He has power to accomplish some desired good. For example, when Solomon prayed for a wise and discerning heart, God freely gave Solomon what he wanted (1 Kings 3). God was delighted that Solomon did not ask for a long life, riches, and success. These are the felt needs of most people in power. Solomon had not treated God as a genie in a lamp who exists to grant him three wishes. What we want by nature—the cravings of the flesh—expresses our sin nature. But Solomon had learned to know what he really needed. He had learned to pray according to the will of God, and it pleased God to answer him. The Lord changes what we want, and we learn to pray for what delights God, to want what He wants.

God challenges the things that everybody, everywhere eagerly pursues (Matt. 6:32). What desires of body and mind (Eph. 2:3) *do* people naturally follow? Consider our characteristic

---

[111] Gal. 5:16-25; Rom. 6:16-18; 8:12-16; Ps. 23:3.

passions: desires of the body include life itself, air, health, water, food, clothing, shelter, sexual pleasure, rest, and exercise. Desires of the mind include happiness, being loved, meaning, money and possessions, respect, status, accomplishment, self-esteem, success, control, power, self-righteousness, aesthetic pleasure, knowledge, marriage and family. Must these rule our lives? They did not rule Jesus' life. Can these cravings really be changed? The Bible says Yes, and points us to the promises of God: to indwell us with power, to write truth on our hearts, to pour out His love in our hearts, to enable us to say "Abba, Father."

As we have seen, many of these things are not bad in themselves. The evil in our desires does not lie in what we want, but in the fact that we want it too much. Our desires for good things seize the throne, becoming idols that replace the King. God refuses to serve our instinctive longings, but commands us to be ruled by other longings. What God commands, He provides the power to accomplish: He works in us both the willing and the doing of His good pleasure (Phil. 2:12-13).

Can you change what you most deeply want? Yes. Does that answer to this question surprise you? It counters influential contemporary views of human motivation. Most Christian counseling books follow on the heels of secular psychologists and take your desires, your "felt needs," as givens. Many leading Christian psychologists make the unchangeability of what we long for the foundation of their systems. For example, many teach that we have an "empty love tank" inside. Our craving for love must be met, or we are doomed to a life of misery and sin. Desires to feel good about ourselves ("self-esteem") or to accomplish something meaningful are similarly baptized. This creates the psychological equivalent of the "Health and Wealth" theology, which similarly selects certain common desires and accepts them as givens that God is obligated to fulfill. The psychological versions of health and wealth miss that God is about the business of changing what people really long for. If felt needs are unchangeable, then it is impossible for us to learn to pray the way Solomon did. This reinforces our tendency to pray for our cravings. It reinforces a sense of victimization in those who were mistreated. It reinforces the tendency to press God into the service of our lusts. Nowhere in the Bible does anyone pray, "Lord, meet my need to feel significant and my need to feel loved." Knowledge of the significance of your life and of the security of God's love for you comes through a different channel than "I long for significance and security."

The deepest longings of the human heart can and must be changed as we are remade into all that God designed us to be. Our deviant longings are illegitimate masters. Even where the object of desire is a good thing, the status of the desire usurps God. Our cravings should be recognized in order that we may more richly know God as the Savior, Lover, and Converter of the human soul. God would have us long for Him more than we long for His gifts. To make us truly human, God must change what we want; we must learn to want the things Jesus wanted. It is no surprise that the psychologists can't find any biblical proof texts for their view of human motivation. The Bible teaches a different view.

The Christian life is a great paradox. Those who die to self, find self. Those who die to their cravings will receive many times as much in this age, and, in the age to come, eternal life (Luke 18:29). They will find new passions worth living for and dying for. If I crave happiness, I will receive misery. If I crave to be loved, I will receive rejection. If I crave significance, I will receive futility. If I crave control, I will receive chaos. If I crave reputation, I will receive humiliation. But if I long for God and His wisdom and mercy, I will receive God and wisdom and mercy. Along the way, sooner or later, I will also receive happiness, love, meaning, order, and glory.

Every vital Christian testifies that the instinctive passions and desires of the flesh can be replaced with the new priorities of the Spirit. This reorientation is not instant and complete, but it is genuine and progressive. Two of the greatest books of practical Christian theology— Augustine's Confessions and Jonathan Edwards's *Treatise Concerning Religious Affections* — meditate exactly on this transformation. And one assumes that Francis of Assisi meant his prayer: "O Divine Master, grant that I may not so much seek to be consoled, as to console; to be understood, as to understand; to be loved, as to love." The craving to learn *how* to love and understand replaces the craving for love and understanding.

Those who hunger and thirst for such righteousness will be satisfied. We have Jesus' word. We have no promise, however, that God will satisfy the instinctive cravings of the soul. The Bible teaches us to pray, to learn to ask for what we really need. Can we pray the petitions of the Lord's Prayer and really mean it? Yes. Can we long for God's glory, for His will to be obeyed, for daily material provision for all God's people, for sins to be forgiven, for aid in warfare with evil? Yes. A wise Puritan pastor, Stephen Charnock, once wrote of "the expulsive power of a new affection." New ruling desires expel lesser masters from the throne. What are the new and different motives that rule in renewed hearts? What changed objects of desire characterize the master motives of the new, listening heart? How does God change what people want? The Bible treats these matters everywhere.[112]

---

[112] The following passages get a start on this question. For each passage ask, "What does this person really want, long for, pursue, delight in?" Ps. 42:1-2; Ps. 63:1-8; Ps. 73:25-28; Ps. 80; Ps. 90:8-17; Prov. 2:1-6; Prov. 3:13-18; Prov. 8:11; Isa. 26:8-9; Matt. 5:6; Matt. 6:9-13; Matt. 6:19-33; Matt. 13:45-46; Luke 11:9-13; Rom. 5:1-11; Rom. 8:18-25; Rom. 9:1-3; 2 Cor. 5:8-9; Phil.1:18-25; Phil. 3:8-11; Phil. 3:20- 21; 2 Tim. 2:22; 2 Tim. 3:12; 1 Peter 1:13; 1 Peter 2:2;

Idolatrous cravings hijack the human heart. Both the Christian life and Christian ministry are by definition about the business of accomplishing a transformation in what people want. Such transformations lie at the center of the Holy Spirit's purposes in working His Word into our lives. The lusts of the flesh lead somewhere bad: dead works. The lusts of the flesh have a specific solution: the gospel of Jesus Christ, which replaces them. "He died for all, so that they who live might no longer live for themselves, but for Him who died and rose again on their behalf" (2 Cor. 5:15). The desires of the Lord lead to somewhere good: good works. One key ingredient in reclaiming the cure of souls is to make this transformation central.

Conclusion

We have probed only one of the many terms by which the Bible explains the workings of the human heart in specific detail. This is a theme whose riches are inexhaustible. The human heart is an active verb. We do not "have needs"; we "do desires," just as we do love, fear, hope, trust, and all the rest. In this article we have examined the verbs of desire. We could have examined any of scores of complementary verbs that capture the fundamental activism of the heart of man. But we would do so confident of this: The gospel of Jesus Christ is as wide as human diversity and as deep as human complexity. The Scriptures that bear witness to this Christ in the power of His Spirit are sufficient to cure souls.

Rev. 22:20.

Chapter 4

Counsel the Sufficient Word
Dr. Heath Lambert

Introduction: The Authoritative and Sufficient Word of God

I suspect the title of this chapter looks odd to many Christians. Christians love the Word of God, and love to lift it high. But what does it mean to *counsel* the Word? Christians are more accustomed to a phrase like *preach* the Word. That idea has much more traction in our Christian culture. We expect a faithful church to engage in faithful preaching, and we get upset if anything less happens. No faithful church would ever tolerate preaching that is subbiblical. A pastor in such a faithful church would be in trouble if he ever said something like, "Would you please turn in your copy of *On the Interpretation of Dreams and Sleep* to page 410? And we will free-associate together for forty-five minutes." If he announced he was going to begin a sermon series expositing *Man's Search for Meaning* by Viktor Frankl, he would probably end up in a very unpleasant meeting afterward. That is because Christians expect our churches to *preach* the Word.

But my concern in this chapter is that so many of those faithful churches do not have a similar concern that we *counsel* the Word. It has been the job of the biblical counseling movement for almost fifty years, and the job of the Association of Certified Biblical Counselors for forty years, to impress upon Christians it is just as important that the Word of God inform the ministry of counseling as it is that it inform the ministry of preaching. I am grateful to God every time Christians are shocked when they hear preaching that falls short of God's Word in the Bible. I am longing for the day when just as many Christians would equally be shocked by counseling that falls short of the Word of God. My goal in this chapter is to help create that sense of shock.

When we think about the doctrine of Scripture, sufficiency is not one of the concepts we often consider. We spend a great deal of time thinking about inspiration, and are ready to fight hard for it. That is good because the Bible *is* inspired. God has breathed out his very own words into the pages of the Bible (2 Tim 3:16-17). We can never negotiate away this crucial truth.

Because the Bible is inspired, it is inerrant. Scripture is perfectly true with no errors. It is a flawless document. If the Bible is God's Word, the only option is its complete truthfulness since it is impossible for God to lie (Heb 6:18). Christians believe in the inerrancy of Scripture due to our confidence in the unimpeachable character of our perfect God.

So, the inspiration of Scripture leads to inerrancy. The inerrancy of Scripture, though, leads to something, as well. The inspired and inerrant Word is also the authoritative Word. If the Bible is God's Word, and God can never lie, then we have a perfect standard to embrace and obey. It is our authority. We do not have the option to reject words that are given to us from the God who never lies. We are required to submit.

I engaged in a formal study of theology for more than eleven years, and have taught in a theological seminary for the same amount of time. During that period, I have observed that Christians typically focus on those precious truths of inspiration, inerrancy, and authority when they discuss the doctrine of Scripture. Another doctrine, however, frequently overlooked, is the doctrine of the sufficiency of Scripture. That doctrine does not receive the attention it deserves.[113] But we must pay attention to

---

[113]As one example of this inattention, I am aware of only one systematic theology textbook that engages in a chapter-length examination of the doctrine

the sufficiency of Scripture because the Bible regularly teaches it. It is ironic that many of the passages Christians use to emphasize the authority of Scripture also include teaching the sufficiency of Scripture so easily overlooked by many (e.g., Psalm 119; 2 Tim 3:1-17; 2 Pet 1:3ff).

The sufficiency of Scripture means that the Bible is rich in resources to address the problems in living we face in this fallen world. It means that God has told us what we need to live life in the midst of the various spiritual and emotional struggles we encounter. The resources available in Scripture for our counseling-related difficulties are not wanting so that they need to be augmented with the resources of, for instance, modern secular therapeutic techniques. This teaching on the sufficiency of Scripture is crucial for a reason closely connected to the authority of Scripture. The sufficiency of Scripture is necessary to demonstrate that the Bible's authority is relevant for our lives. Think for a moment about the significance of this issue.

It would be possible for the Bible to be authoritative, and abstract. In such a situation, the Bible would speak with complete authority concerning matters that are tangential to human life. For example, God could have given us a Bible that explains the details of the molecular composition of the sun. If God inspired a Bible with this information, we would have confidence that the information was true. We would trust that information as authoritative. We would also have to admit, however, that it is irrelevant for living life in a world with suicide, Parkinson's disease, and temptations to commit sexual sin.

God did not give us that kind of Bible. He gave us a Bible that relates to the lives we live on this planet. The Bible includes

---

of sufficiency. See Wayne Grudem, *Systematic Theology* (Grand Rapids: Zondervan, 2000), 127-40.

information about responding to grief and overcoming temptations to sin. The Lord instructs us regarding how we can have hope when life threatens to overwhelm us with despair. God shares the details about how to respond to paralyzing fear in a world that can scare us to death. Scripture maps out strategies to resolve conflicts with our spouse, to extend love to someone we do not like, and to walk with a friend down the hard road of a terminal illness. The Bible speaks to these and thousands of other issues that we face in actual life. The Bible is authoritative, and its authority is relevant to what we deal with in our lives. That is what the biblical counseling movement has meant by sufficiency, and is the reason we have argued for it so persistently.

What I want to impress here, then, is that the inspired, inerrant, and authoritative Word is the *sufficient* Word, as well. In order for God's Word to be compelling and relevant, it must be authoritative and sufficient. My goal in the rest of this chapter is to show from 2 Peter why we must be committed to counseling this authoritative and sufficient Word.

Counseling the Sufficient Word: Four Arguments from 2 Peter 1

Second Peter 1 is a chapter in Scripture pertaining to the Word of God. In glorious terms, the apostle Peter presents an argument for the inspiration, inerrancy, authority, and sufficiency of Scripture. In making such a case, he buttresses the confidence Christians can have, not just in Scripture in general, but in the inspiration, inerrancy, authority, and sufficiency of Scripture for counseling. I want to make four observations with respect to counseling from Peter's argument in 2 Peter 1.

The Subject Matter of Scripture Is the Subject Matter of Counseling

The issues on the table in counseling are the problems that plague us as we live life in a fallen world. The examples of these problems are impossible to count, but include marriage conflict, pornography, overwhelming depression, overpowering anger, paralyzing anxiety, confusion with regard to decisions both large and small, sorrow about children who have gone astray, difficulties dealing with parents who hate you, the pain of financial pressure, the complex management of extreme mood swings, stress over a lost job, and numerous others. People seek counseling help when they encounter problems like these.

The logic driving a quest for counseling is not just the presence of a problem, but the need for assistance. People do not seek counseling for just *any* problem. They pursue counseling when they have not been able to address those problems on their own. Counseling happens when individuals with problems realize that the difficulty is too much for them and discover they need help. In fact, we can say this more strongly. Counseling occurs when someone is overwhelmed by a problem and realizes the need, not just for help, but for *power*.

The reality is that, when we face the kinds or problems addressed in counseling, we require more than mere help in the form of advice or practical tips for living. People in real trouble know that, when problems overwhelm us, we need real power to break their hold. Consider a married couple seeking counseling after years of conflict, emotional manipulation, and adulterous relationships have caused love to grow stale. Now neither member of the couple can remember what it was like to feel affection for the other, and quitting seems the easiest thing to do, but they decide to give counseling a shot, realizing what they really need is a miracle.

Or, consider a 24-year-old man whose engagement just ended after his fiancé got sick of his porn addiction. He has been watching pornography on the Internet since he was five years old, and has tried to quit many times with no success. He has listened to his parents, his roommate, and his girlfriend encourage him to quit, but has never found it possible. Now, discouraged, he takes a crack at counseling, but recognizes that deep down something amazing must happen to break the hold of porn in his life.

Whether the problems concern marriage, pornography, or something else, individuals with real problems know they need something more than techniques to really change. The quest for counseling is the search for power in the face of debilitating difficulties.

That is why it is such tremendously good news to read these words in 2 Peter 1:3-4:

> His divine power has granted to us all things that pertain to life and godliness, through the knowledge of him who called us to his own glory and excellence, by which he has granted to us his precious and very great promises, so that through them you may become partakers of the divine nature, having escaped from the corruption that is in the world because of sinful desire.

In a world where people stand in desperate need of power as they confront overwhelming problems, the apostle Peter says God gives his divine power for every hardship we face that pertains to life and godliness.

The divine power granted to us when we face trouble is quite personal. It is the power of Jesus himself, who was just addressed in 2 Peter 1:2. The infinite value of this passage is that Jesus Christ himself shows up in our problems to give us his personal power. But how is this power of Jesus communicated? The text tells us that it is *through the knowledge of him who called us to his own glory and excellence,* and that it comes by *precious and very great promises.* This language is a clear reference to Scripture. Second Peter promises that God gives the power of Christ to Christians when they face difficulties in this life, and that he communicates that power through the Scriptures.

People seek out counseling when they are troubled with problems in their lives. God provides power to overcome these problems through the grace of his Son, Jesus, and he explains how to access that power in the Bible. This all means that the topics addressed in counseling conversations are the same topics God unpacks in Scripture. The biblical counseling position on the sufficiency of Scripture for counseling is, therefore, nothing more or less than simple faith in the love of God to give us powerful grace in the midst of trouble, and to explain how to access that grace in the pages of Scripture.

But this position has aroused great concern from many. Throughout the history of the biblical counseling movement, numerous critics have been concerned that this argument claims too much for Scripture. They are concerned that biblical counselors will overlook true information existing outside Scripture. One such thoughtful critic is Stanton Jones.

In an article he wrote for a book titled, *Psychology and Christianity: Five Views,* Jones argues against the sufficiency of Scripture for counseling with the following statement: "There are many topics to which Scripture does not speak: how neurons work, how the brain synthesizes mathematical or emotional information, the types of memory or the best way to characterize personality traits."[114] Jones's point is that the Bible cannot be sufficient for counseling if it is missing information like this. In evaluating Jones's claim, we need to be honest that he is correct in one sense, and incorrect in another sense.

Jones is correct that information such as how neurons work and the kinds of memories human beings possess are not in the Bible. I am aware of no passage of Scripture addressing any of these issues—certainly not in the kind of detail that would be appealing to experts in these areas. The Bible certainly speaks with authority about every physical issue of the human body that it addresses, but it makes no claim to be comprehensively sufficient for the kind of physical care that is the concern, for example, of medical doctors. Jones is thus correct that the Bible is a limited book, and does not include all manner of information of tremendous importance, and of great interest to many people.

But as correct as Jones is regarding that matter, he is incorrect about something much more important to the counseling task. He is incorrect about the subject matter of counseling. In arguing about the insufficiency of Scripture for the discipline of counseling, Jones lists all sorts of topics that Scripture does not cover (e.g., synthesizing mathematical information, and characterizing personality traits) but, in building this list, he avoids including topics that actually are discussed in counseling. The issues Jones lists as not being covered in Scripture are also subjects that are not addressed in counseling.

The items on Jones's list are not topics that any counselor—biblical or secular—brings up in counseling because they are not the subjects that really help with the problems people bring into counseling. Consider the members of that married couple I

---

[114] Stanton Jones, "An Integration View," in *Psychology and Christianity: Five Views*, ed. Eric L. Johnson (Downers Grove: InterVarsity Press, 2010), 116.

mentioned who pursue counseling after years of marriage trouble. No one thinks the solution to their problem is found in an explanation of the synthesis of mathematical information. Or think of the man enslaved to pornography. No counselor would try to help him with an explanation of ways neurons work in the brain.[115]

It is simply missing the point to insist that the Bible must include information about these realities to be sufficient for counseling. No biblical counselor denies that these realities are true, or that they are relevant for many fields. The issue is that such realities are not what is addressed in counseling. Because these realities do not come up in counseling, their absence in Scripture is not evidence that the Bible is insufficient for counseling conversations.

Peter's argument is that God reveals in Scripture what we need to know for addressing problems we face as we live life and pursue godliness. These are the topics addressed in counseling. The Lord does not need to furnish us with exhaustive information about every item in the field of psychology to keep his promise to reveal in Scripture his power for our problems.

The Journey of the Christian Life Is the Journey of Counseling

I have been maintaining that counseling happens when people experience problems in a fallen world that are so serious they cannot deal with them on their own. These difficulties have

---

[115] This statement is true even though the activity of neurons in the brain is necessary to process pornographic images. See, William Struthers, *Wired for Intimacy: How Pornography Hijacks the Male Brain* (Downer's Grove: InterVarsity Press, 2009). Even though neurons are involved at a physiological level, these categories are not the most helpful ones to discuss in counseling. See, Heath Lambert, *A Theology of Biblical Counseling: The Doctrinal Foundations of Counseling Ministry* (Grand Rapids: Zondervan, 2016), 93-97.

ground their life to a halt, and they can no longer function without assistance and intervention. The apostle Peter refers to people in this state as being "ineffective or unfruitful" (2 Pet 1:8). Based on this language, we could say that counseling is a journey to restore people rendered ineffective and unfruitful by trouble to effectiveness and fruitfulness in life and godliness. And the Bible does not leave us to guess about how to travel on this journey, but rather tells us explicitly how to do it.

In particular, we are told, "If these qualities are yours and are increasing, they keep you from being ineffective or unfruitful in the knowledge of our Lord Jesus Christ" (2 Pet 1:8). Certain qualities, when possessed by Christians, work against the debilitating ineffectiveness and unfruitfulness of trouble. These qualities are the eight listed in the verses immediately preceding 2 Peter 1:8,

> Make every effort to supplement your faith with virtue, and virtue with knowledge, and knowledge with self-control, and self-control with steadfastness, and steadfastness with godliness, and godliness with brotherly affection, and brotherly affection with love (2 Pet 1:5-7).

The list of qualities begins with faith. The reason is that "without faith it is impossible to please him [God]" (Heb 11:6). The fountainhead of every virtue is faith. It makes all the other virtues possible because we have no access to God and his grace that produces every other virtue apart from faith in his Son. But once faith has been wrought in our hearts by the gift of God's grace (Eph 2:8), it brings with it the other virtues of the Christian life.

So, as a demonstration of faith, Christians must make every effort to supplement their faith with virtue, or moral excellence. They need to bolster their virtue with knowledge, which means the knowledge of God as they grow to know him more fully. To this knowledge, Christians are to add self-control, which is the ability to restrain passions and respond "no" to the flesh. Steadfastness, or persistence and long-suffering, must be added to self-control. Then comes godliness, which literally means being like God, and is an outgrowth of growing in the knowledge of God. To this godliness should be added love for Christian brothers and sisters, and to that is added a general attitude of love for all people.

Peter is making the very important point that the overflow of the Christian faith is the Christian life. Belief in the gospel of Jesus Christ produces a life of virtue that grows in Christ-likeness, demonstrating itself in the fruits of the repentant life of faith. Peter is spelling out what Paul refers to as "the obedience of faith" (Rom 1:5). The working out of all these qualities is a journey. Peter says that we "supplement" our faith or "add to" it. This process happens slowly and over time (2 Cor 3:18).

The point of all this in a chapter regarding the sufficiency of Scripture for counseling clarifies that Christians' journey, as they live the Christian life, is the same journey on which biblical counselors want to lead troubled people. Peter makes clear in his letter that these qualities—which constitute his summary of the journey of the Christian life—are the same qualities that, when absent from our life, lead to the ineffectiveness and unfruitfulness characterizing the problems leading people to seek counseling. According to Peter, it is the qualities characterizing a faithful Christian life that serve as the solutions to the problems, which lead people to seek counseling. The Christian journey of faithful living in a fallen world, is the same journey that solves the ineffectiveness and unfruitfulness in the lives of those who require counseling.

Consequently, the job of biblical counselors is to be experts at living the Christian life and helping others to live it, as well. A biblical counselor is one who knows, with wisdom and skill, how to

131

help someone journey through the Christian life at the precise point this journey has become problematic. Counseling problems happen when individuals are not growing in the faith of Christ, and effective counselors will be skilled at diagnosing these difficulties and helping troubled people walk out specific change. It is at this point we can begin to understand an objection that is frequently leveled at biblical counselors.

In the previous section, I dealt with those who object to biblical counseling based on the resources available to counselors as they do their work. Here the concern pertains to the facility of counselors as they attempt to minister to troubled people. To help explain the critical distinction between resources and facility, it will help to tell a story about the day my wife woke up with the flu.

On this terrible morning, it was seconds after I learned my wife was ill that I learned my children were hungry, too. Trying to remain calm, I headed down the stairs, seated the children at the breakfast table, and opened the door to the pantry. What I saw was horrifying. There was plenty of food in the pantry but, as I looked at boxes, cans, bags of flour, and heaven-knows-what-else, I met a crushing realization: I had no idea how my wife was able to transform all that packaged stuff into the food we ate once she set it on the table. I looked from the pantry to the six, pouting eyes staring at me, and I made a decision made by countless fathers since the dawn of the modern world: I went to McDonald's.

If you understand this story, you recognize the difference between resources and facility. I had more than enough resources in my pantry that morning to prepare a delightful breakfast for my children. The problem was that I did not have my wife's facility to transform those resources into something consumable by my children. It is the same way with the Bible and counseling. We have more than enough scriptural resources to assist any troubled person whom the Lord would send our way. What we are often missing is the facility to share those resources with folks who are experiencing trouble in a manner that leads to help.

This difficulty becomes a powerful objection to the biblical counseling movement when people with serious problems meet with "counselors" with no real skill in connecting the Bible to their problems in meaningful ways that lead to assistance. I have heard too many stories about broken individuals receiving tragic counsel from those who believed wonderful things about the Bible, but who never took the time to grow in the skills necessary to offer precise biblical care. The existence of this problem is an encouragement for all Christians to increase in the facility required to provide true care to people stuck on the journey of the Christian life. If we fail here, we will slander the sufficient resources God has given us in Scripture.

The Apostolic Commitment to Scripture Is the Biblical Counseling Commitment to Scripture

Peter knows that the qualities of a fruitful faith work, over time, to neutralize the ineffectiveness and unfruitfulness of the problems we face in a fallen world. Furthermore, he knows that Scripture authoritatively unpacks how to take hold of these qualities. Because of that, Peter has an unrelenting commitment to the use of Scripture in his ministry.

I intend always to remind you of these qualities, though you know them and are established in the truth that you have. I think it right, as long as I am in this body, to stir you up by way of reminder, since I know that the putting off of my body will be soon, as our Lord Jesus Christ made clear to me. And I will make every effort so that after my departure you may be able at any time to recall these things (2 Pet 1:12-15).

Peter knows the principles the Lord reveals to Christians in a fallen world address the categories that create trouble in our lives, requiring counsel. And so he exerts "every effort" to make his contribution to the Christian Scriptures, so that God's people will have the resources to deal with the problems they are facing.

On three occasions in this text, Peter discusses how important it is for them to remember the truth of God that counteracts their problems in living: *I intend always to remind you of these qualities . . . . I think it is right, as long as I am in this body, to stir you up by way of reminder . . . . I will make every effort so that after my departure you may be able at any time to recall these things.* Peter understands that those in the throes of problems need the truth of God. He knows they need to be reminded of the truth even when they have heard it previously. And so he works to give it to them.

Biblical counselors have this same commitment as they do their work of caring for hurting and troubled individuals. We know that God has given us a Word, the contents of which intersect directly with the trouble people bring into counseling. Biblical counselors are committed to utilizing the Scriptures in counseling as a demonstration of relevant compassion for those in desperate need of practical care that leads to genuine change.

Other counseling approaches adopted by Christians do not share this commitment. Other approaches to counseling argue that the Scriptures should not occupy so central a role in the counseling relationship. One person who holds this position is Mark McMinn. He is one of the leading scholars today advocating an integration approach to counseling, which minimizes the use of

Scripture in counseling.[116]   McMinn wrote a very influential book, called *Psychology, Theology, and Spirituality in Christian Counseling*. In the book, he writes a chapter about Scripture and how to employ it in counseling. He starts the chapter with a crucial question: "Should Christians use Scripture in counseling or not?"[117] That is a question of vital importance, and McMinn answers it with a great deal of suspicion about the use of the Bible in counseling.   He begins a response with a caution about using Scripture. "We may rely excessively on Scripture when we could be using other counseling strategies: cognitive therapy strategies can be quickly and effectively applied to panic disorders; behavioral strategies reduce phobic reactions. If we rely too heavily on Scripture, we may miss other valid treatment options."[118]   Further on, he says, "Psychological competence in counseling is important. The best counselors use Scripture only after carefully considering the psychological implications and the effect on the therapeutic relationship."[119]   He adds, "At this time, the research is so limited, that it is premature to draw any conclusions about the effective use of Scripture in counseling."[120]   By the end of the chapter, he

---

[116] Lest this statement sound unfairly harsh, it is an observation made by McMinn himself. He cites a study from the Christian Association for Psychological Studies (CAPS), showing that only about 3 percent of the members of that organization directly use Scripture in their counseling work. McMinn notes, "Thus, it appears that directly using Scripture as part of counseling is relatively rare, even among Christian counselors." See Mark R. McMinn, *Psychology, Theology, and Spirituality in Christian Counseling* (Wheaton: Tyndale, 1996), 99.

[117] Ibid., 97.

[118] Ibid., 115.

[119] Ibid., 116.

[120] Ibid., 122.

remarks, "Using Scripture in counseling introduces the risk of significantly reducing client freedom by imposing the therapist's values on the client. Religious psychotherapy, in general, introduces the risks of imposing unwanted values or beliefs on a client, and explicitly using Scripture in counseling quickly magnifies the risk."[121]

I want to be clear at this point that Mark McMinn is my friend and brother in Christ. I have spent time getting to know him; I pray for him and his family regularly; and I care for him very deeply. I have found him to be one of the most kind and generous people I have ever met. And yet, I must express concern at his published statements about the use of Scripture in counseling. The problem with them is that they simply do not sound apostolic. When the apostle Peter was confronted with troubled people in need of counseling, he made every effort to remind them of the truths of Scripture, which he believed would restore them to effectiveness and fruitfulness. When McMinn addresses these same counseling issues, he is concerned about an excessive use of Scripture, the lack of research showing the effectiveness of Scripture, and the risks of an excessive use of Scripture. These concerns are ultimately at odds with a uniquely Christian commitment to Scripture.

As Christians, we are people of the book. We are fundamentally committed to the Word of God. This commitment must extend to the conversations we have. Whether we call these conversations evangelism, discipleship, lunch at Wendy's, talking with a neighbor in the backyard, counseling, or even psychotherapy, God has not allowed Christians the option of having conversations that are not grounded in and do not point to

---

[121] Ibid.

the Word of God.   All Christians must pray that we would strengthen our commitment to the Bible—not weaken it.

The Authority of Scripture Is the Authority in Counseling

The apostle Peter ends the first chapter of his second epistle with two stunning claims. Following is the first one:

> For we did not follow cleverly devised myths when we made known to you the power and coming of our Lord Jesus Christ, but we were eyewitnesses of his majesty. For when he received honor and glory from God the Father, and the voice was borne to him by the Majestic Glory, "This is my beloved Son, with whom I am well pleased," we ourselves heard this very voice borne from heaven, for we were with him on the holy mountain (2 Pet 1:16-18).

Peter is making the breathtaking claim that when Jesus's glory ripped through the humility of his human form, Peter and the other apostles saw it with their own eyes.

His claim is one of eyewitness testimony that the biblical authors often make (cf., 1 Cor 15:5-8; 1 John 1:1-3). The apostles and prophets who penned Scripture issue a steadfast denial to the charge that they were engaging in the spread of mythology or fairy tales. The apostles went to their death insisting that the event about which they wrote happened in actual history, and that they had seen these occurrences with their own eyes. Such assertions give us confidence that God's revelation in the Bible is built on historical fact, rather than the stuff of legend.

After this, Peter makes another stunning claim. The episode on the Mount of Transfiguration is actual history corroborated by his own eyewitness testimony. And yet, Christians today have a level of certainty in the historicity of this event even beyond Peter's firsthand reporting of it. He goes on to say,

> We have the prophetic word more fully confirmed, to which you will do well to pay attention as to a lamp shining in a dark place, until the day dawns and the morning star rises in your hearts (2 Pet 1:19).

Peter again encourages Christians to pay continual attention to Scripture. Indeed, he wants us to use Scripture like a lamp in a dark place (cf., Ps 119:105) until the day dawns and the morning star rises, which is a reference to the second coming of Christ (cf., Phil 1:6, 10; 2:16; 1 Thess 5:2). Peter makes the astounding contention that we should pay such careful attention to Scripture because the testimony of the Word of God is more certain than is Peter's own eyewitness testimony: *We have the prophetic word more fully confirmed.* That means you can be more sure that biblical events like the transfiguration happened because you read about them in the Bible than you could be if you had been present yourself and had seen them with your own eyes.

Peter then proceeds to provide an explanation about why we can have such certainty in the testimony of the Word of God.

> No prophecy of Scripture comes from someone's own interpretation. For no prophecy was ever produced by the will of man, but men spoke from God as they were carried along by the Holy Spirit (2 Pet 1:20-21).

This is a biblical example of the doctrine of accommodation. Accommodation is the way God preserves the inerrant quality of the Scriptures without losing the individual personality of the human authors who compose the text. The doctrine means that

God uses human beings as legitimate agents in the creation of the biblical text; they compose exactly what he wants them to write, while still preserving their individual experiences and expressions. God accommodates the personalities of the human authors in ways that preserve the message he wants to be communicated. The men speak, but the Lord carries them along as they do so. God inspires the Scriptures, using the means of accommodation.

This explains why Peter wants us to possess so much confidence in Scripture's authority to communicate history. We can trust the biblical accounts of history even more than we can rely on the eyewitness account Peter. The reason for this is that, as soon as the Holy Spirit inspired Peter to write down his eyewitness account, Peter ceased being a lone witness, and God the Spirit himself became a witness. This means, quite frankly, that if you had the choice of traveling back in time and seeing the biblical events yourself, or of reading about them in the Bible, you should choose to read the Scriptures if what you want is complete certainty. The memory of human witness could be faulty, but God's testimony will never fail (1 Pet 1:24-25).

Peter's argument here is powerful. According to him, Scripture powerfully addresses the problems we face in this world, and he shows us a biblical process to address the difficulties. Because of this reality, we should pay constant attention to Scripture until the day dawns and the darkness of problems in a fallen world goes away forever. But at this point in his argument Peter does something incredible. He wants us to have confidence in this relevant Bible, to which we must pay attention. And so he makes a powerful statement about the authority of Scripture. He holds that Scripture does not constitute just the words of man, but the words of God himself. In this way, Peter seeks to uphold our confidence in the authority of the Bible for addressing the trouble we face.

Biblical counselors embrace this understanding of the relevant authority of Scripture. It is on the authority of 2 Peter 1, that biblical counselors believe that the use of the Scriptures in counseling is not merely about the sufficiency of Scripture, but also the authority of Scripture. This issue of authority answers another objection made against biblical counselors.

A few years ago, a reporter from the *Pacific Standard Magazine* interviewed me for an article being written about the biblical counseling movement. When the article was released, I was fascinated by this statement by the article's author,

> In [biblical counselor's] attempts to cast aside the many shortcomings and contradictions of psychiatry and psychology, Jay Adams and others wound up creating many problems of their own. How can you decry the ineffectiveness of psychiatry in treating mental disorders yet contend that effectiveness is beside the point in biblical counseling?[122]

The author of the piece, Kathryn Joyce, is making quite a provocative point with this question. She is correct in stating that biblical counselors have frequently pointed to the many failures of secular therapy in making a defense of counseling that is uniquely biblical. Joyce takes that argument and turns it on counselors committed to the sufficiency and authority of Scripture. She maintains that, unless biblical counseling has a 100 percent success rate, it is hypocritical to identify the failures of others as evidence that their approaches do not work. How can biblical counselors

---

[122] Kathryn Joyce, "The Rise of Biblical Counseling" psmag.com. https://psmag.com/the-rise-of-biblical-counseling-7af9da5b00d0#.w03lly4i8 (accessed August 1, 2014).

criticize failure when they experience it themselves? This critique of biblical counseling is as fair as it is important.

The answer to the criticism requires an understanding of the kind of biblical authority that Peter teaches in his letter. On our way to discussing this authority, we should be honest that all biblical counselors who have highlighted secular counseling failures have additionally experienced failure in their own ministry. Nobody bats a thousand, not even with a commitment to Scripture.

Counseling failure is no respecter of persons, and does not privilege select counseling approaches. Every counselor—from the staunchest atheist to the most devout follower of Christ—has felt the sting of watching a counselee leave unchanged. Biblical counselors have not focused on the failures of secular counseling in a hypocritical effort to paper over their own shortcomings. Instead, the biblical counseling critique about secular therapy has had less to do with the fact *that* it has failed, and has had more to do with *how* it has failed.

Secular counselors, and the Christians who depend on their therapies for their own work, have chosen counseling systems that reject the authority of the Bible in the counseling room. This rejection of biblical authority guarantees that their counseling approaches can never succeed in any ultimate way. Their counseling failures are obvious and easy examples of the failure of their approach. But the reality is that, even when their counseling has the appearance of success, it is an illustration of the failure of their approach because the changes produced are not ones that honor Christ.[123]

---

[123] There is more to say about this issue than I can manage in this space, but I go into much additional detail about it in Lambert, *A Theology of Biblical Counseling*, 18-25.

To have a chance at counseling success, we must have a commitment to biblical authority. Once we sit under the inspired, inerrant, authoritative, and sufficient Scriptures, we have God's standard for how counseling should work, and goals it should possess. Counselors who embrace this authority will still experience failure. (Our own human limitations and weaknesses too often lead us to misunderstand the problems of counselees; we can misapply biblical truth in our efforts at care; and our counselees can be hard-hearted, rejecting even our most faithful efforts.) But when counseling still fails due to human error in the counseling process, biblical counselors can have confidence in our model because it rests on God's authoritative Word.

On the contrary, even when secular counseling "succeeds," it eventually counts as failure because the model is fundamentally about making people feel better without God. Their source of authority is their own wisdom, and so they can never attain the kind of change that God desires, and which matters for eternity. Their obvious counseling failures demonstrate their flawed model in an obvious and immediate way, but a careful examination shows that even their triumphs fail to produce the kind of change that matters in the long haul.

The real issue is not whether we ever experience counseling failure—that is inescapable in a fallen world. The heart of the matter is whether we embrace a model of counseling that rests on the authority of God: explaining life the way he sees it, understanding our problems according to his perspective, and charting solutions in keeping with his wisdom. If we reject biblical authority, our counseling can never ultimately succeed. If we embrace it, we can rely on that authority to correct us and help us improve even when we fail by falling short of that authority.

Counseling the Sufficient Word: A Case Study

We can know that the Scriptures are sufficient for counseling because of the teaching of 2 Peter that the Bible speaks with relevant authority into the problems leading individuals to seek out counseling. But, in the face of the dynamic stories we encounter with actual lives of real people experiencing painful problems, such an argument can sometimes seem abstract. This is the reason I have frequently maintained that case studies about real counselees are so significant in demonstrating the omni-relevance of the Scriptures to the problems we face. When you see how the Bible springs into the life of a troubled person—highlighting the grace of Jesus, who brings personal change—it becomes hard, if not impossible, to deny the Scripture's sufficiency in counseling.

I want to drive home all I have said with regard to the Bible and counseling in 2 Peter by telling you the story of a woman named Elva. She was in her seventies, and had been widowed after her husband lost his battle with cancer. Following her husband's death, Elva very quickly became a lonely, angry, and embittered woman. She was always unhappy, always complaining, and always in a bad mood. One day, right in the midst of all this misery, Elva was mugged by a man on the street, who tried to snatch her purse. In the aftermath of this attack, Elva came unglued. Elva had been miserable after her husband's death, but had been able to hold her life together. The mugging changed all that. Elva suddenly felt her mortality and her loneliness in a way that caused her to plummet into depression. At this point, Elva knew she required help, and she sought it in counseling.

I have never met Elva. I learned about her from her secular therapist, Irvin D. Yalom, in a best-selling book he wrote titled, *Love's Executioner and Other Tales of Psychotherapy*. Yalom, who was the professor of psychiatry at Stanford University, had a thriving counseling practice for years. *Love's Executioner* is Yalom's effort to relate the true stories of people whom he tried to help in his counseling practice. Yalom spends a considerable amount of time discussing his counseling relationship with this sad, angry, lonely, scared woman whom he calls Elva, who is overwhelmed by age, loss, pain, and fear. The following is the last page of his story about her.

"The robbery brings home the fact that your husband is really gone."
Her eyes filled with tears, but I felt that I had the right, the mandate to continue. "You knew that before, I know. But part of you didn't. Now you really know that he's dead. He's not in the yard. He's not out back in the workshop. He's not anywhere. Except in your memories."

Elva was really crying now, and her stubby frame heaved with sobs for several minutes. She had never done that before with me. I sat there and wondered, "Now what do I do?" But my instincts luckily led me to what proved to be an inspired gambit. My eyes lit upon her purse— that same ripped-off, much-abused purse; and I said, "Bad luck is one thing, but aren't you asking for it, carrying around something that large?" Elva, plucky as ever, did not fail to call attention to my overstuffed pockets and the clutter on the table next to my chair. She pronounced the purse "medium-sized."

"Any larger," I responded, "and you'd need a luggage carrier to move it around."

"Besides," she said, ignoring my jibe, "I need everything in it."
"You've got to be joking. Let's see!"

Getting into the spirit of it, Elva hoisted her purse onto my table, opened its jaws wide and began to empty it. The first items fetched forth were three empty doggie bags.

"Need two extra ones in case of an emergency?" I asked.

144

Elva chuckled and continued to disembowel the purse. Together we inspected and discussed each item. Elva conceded that the three packets of Kleenex and twelve pens (plus three pencil stubs) were indeed superfluous, but held firm about two bottles of cologne, three hairbrushes, and dismissed, with an imperious flick of her hand, my challenge to her large flashlight, bulky notepads, and huge sheath of photographs.

We quarreled over everything. The roll of fifty dimes. Three bags of candies (low-calorie, of course). She giggled at my question: "Do you believe, Elva, that the more of these you eat the thinner you will become?" A plastic sack of large orange peels ("You never know, Elva, when these will come in handy"). A bunch of knitting needles ("Six needles in search of a sweater," I thought). A bag of sourdough starter. Half of a paperback Stephen King novel (Elva threw away sections of pages as she read them: "They weren't worth keeping," she explained). A small stapler ("Elva, this is crazy!"). Three pairs of sunglasses. And tucked away into the innermost corners, assorted coins, paper clips, nail clippers, pieces of emery board and some substance that looked suspiciously like lint.

When the great bag finally yielded all, Elva and I stared in wonderment at the contents set out in rows on my table. We were sorry the bag was empty and that the emptying was over. She turned and smiled, and we looked tenderly at each other. It was an extraordinarily intimate moment. In a way that a client had never done before, she showed me everything. And I had accepted everything and asked for even more. I followed her into every nook and crevice, awed that one old woman's purse could serve as a vehicle for isolation and intimacy: the absolute isolation that is integral to existence and the intimacy that dispels the dread, if not the fact, of isolation.

That was a transforming hour. Our time of intimacy—call it love, call it lovemaking—was redemptive. In that one hour, Elva moved

from a position of forsakenness to one of trust. She came alive and was
persuaded, once more, of her capacity for intimacy.
I think it was the best hour of therapy I ever gave.[124]

This is an absolutely fascinating account of secular counseling. I share it here because of Yalom's last statement, "*I think it was the best hour of therapy I ever gave.*" When we engage this account, we are engaging Yalom, by his own testimony, at his best. He believes this is the very best he has to offer. It is an example of "successful" secular therapy.

There are some good things to say about Yalom's interaction with Elva. He engaged this woman in a truly sensitive human interaction. His description of their back-and-forth suggests authenticity, humor, candor, and real tenderness. Those are good things for which we can be thankful. In the main, though, we would have to admit that this counseling experience—the best Yalom feels he has ever had—is a tragic failure. By the end of their time together, they have experienced an emptied purse, and a few light laughs. Not much else.

The intimacy Yalom alleges is a counterfeit of the authentic variety that would require addressing issues that really matter in candid and profound ways. The "redemptive" quality of the time that moved Elva from "forsakenness to trust" simply has not come close to happening in anything approximating biblical categories. As a matter of fact, when Elva left Yalom's office that day, the chuckles they shared did nothing to put her life in perspective, to comfort her in the midst of the loss of her husband, to give her hope as her own life comes closer to ending, or to help her know peace in a scary world where men try to steal your purse simply

---

[124] Irvin D. Yalom, *Love's Executioner and Other Tales of Psychotherapy* (New York: Harper Perennial, 1989), 150-51.

146

because you were in the wrong place at the wrong time. Real counseling success—change that *really* helps Elva and honors God—is nowhere in sight from this account.

By standing on God's authoritative and sufficient Word, we can say that biblical counselors on a bad day can do better than the best day of secular counseling. Biblical counselors can explain to Elva everything she most needs to hear, that she has no hope of learning from Yalom. Yalom did not say to Elva—because he does not know—that God has provided a Savior for Elva, who gives her his own power to overcome her anger, fear, and loneliness through faith in him. Because Yalom does not know God's truth, he could not tell her that there is a glorious reality called the Christian life, in which Elva can supplement her faith with the virtues of Christ himself that, slowly and over time, drive out the struggles she is facing. Yalom's inability to see the riches of the Word of God makes it impossible for him to tell Elva how crucial it is for her to press into the pages of Scripture, so that the truth of God's Word can begin to drive away the despairing lies she learned from a lost world. And Elva never learned to have confidence in this authoritative Word to help her because she did not have a counselor whose words overflowed from his own confidence in that Word. The best Elva's therapist had to give her is not worth comparing with what she could have received from someone committed to the Scriptures.

To be clear, I am not upset with Yalom for failing to share things it was impossible for him to share. Yalom is a lost man. His eyes are closed to the truth of the Bible, and his ears are stopped from hearing the beautiful music of the gospel of the grace of Jesus. We should expect Yalom to say things like what he said to Elva. We should not expect that those who know Christ and believe the Bible will look to Yalom, a secular therapist, as one who has access to a glorious deposit of counseling resources that biblical counselors lack.

As biblical counselors, we have it all! God has held nothing back! When you consider all that Jesus has done for troubled individuals, and everything that God has revealed about his work, you discover the real debate in counseling should not concern the sufficiency of *Scripture* for counseling. The actual debate should be the sufficiency of *secular therapy* for counseling. It is secular therapists who operate at a deficit of counseling resources—not Christians. As believers, we possess the inspired, inerrant, authoritative, and sufficient Scripture that makes us more than competent to counsel. What more could we ever want? What more could God ever give?

The Journal of Biblical Counseling

The Journal of Biblical Counseling is a publication of the Christian Counseling and Education Foundation. It addresses today's counseling issues in ways that have lasting relevance and connects God's Word with life and ministry in three issues published a year.

Individual Subscriptions
Digital ($12/year) Print ($27/year)
Institutional Subscriptions
Print ($35/year)
For more information and to subscribe, visit ccef.org/bc

Christian Counseling and Education Foundation
1803 E. Willow Grove Ave., Glenside, PA 19038

ACBC Certification

For nearly 40 years, the *Association of Certified Biblical Counselors* have been training and certifying biblical counselors. Our process is made up of three phases: learning, exams and application, and supervision. For more resources and information on certification, visit www.biblicalcounseling.com.

Made in the USA
Columbia, SC
16 December 2018